I absolutely love anything that opens up my mind. Lara's book does just that. **She takes the task of unthinking 50 years of self-defeating talk and makes it relatable.** AND Lara is funny! This is an easy read that will leave you feeling better about yourself without feeling that you have to change who you are as a person. It changes the way you are with yourself, which changes the way you are in the world.

— **Darlene Turriff,**
author and coach

I recognized myself on every page. Reading it was one huge a-ha moment after another. It gives voice to the nagging thoughts in my head about how I work and why my "downtime" is vital to recharge. Getting lost in thought is NOT a bad thing, especially when you know how to go with it. You're Not Lazy is a wake-up call and an invitation to stop fighting your natural rhythm and start enjoying the unique way you move through life and still meet your BIG goals.

— **Nicole Washburn,**
author and coach

Praise for You're Not Lazy

In *You're Not Lazy*, **Wellman lays out a solid case for rejecting hustle culture and learning to love our brains for what they *can* do.** Wellman deftly reflects the many questions, feelings and anxieties we have about trying to exist in an attention economy that pushes productivity at all costs. By challenging overly critical self-talk and building alternative frameworks for self-appreciation, *You're Not Lazy* is an engaging antidote to the grind.

– **Tracey Lindeman,**
author of *BLEED: Destroying Myths
and Misogyny in Endometriosis Care*

In a culture that constantly asks us to hustle harder and improve, Lara Wellman leads us to a truer truth: **That resting isn't lazy, and that we're not broken if we don't (or can't) live up to society's unrealistic expectations of us.** With her witty and down-to-earth approach, Lara gave me permission to let go of the idea that work needs to be hard for me to find success and meaning in life.

– **Misty Pratt,**
author of *All In Her Head: How Gender Bias
Harms Women's Mental Health*

Our different brains and bodies impact the way we connect with the world, and how the world connects with us. **If you want to rest when everyone says go—or forge a life you'll enjoy more, in small steps that don't require big changes—*You're Not Lazy* will coach you with care.** The book starts with reframing that moment you're on the couch binge-watching a show as being the best place to be ... and builds from there. Take it from a long-time client and friend of Lara's: respecting your energy, as she will show you how to do, will bring you and your community far.

– Elizabeth Howell,
science and space journalist

At least once a week, I quote Lara's book to someone. **If you're a person who regularly says mean things to yourself about how you don't get enough done and you're failing at life, this book will help you.** Lara is incredible at being able to see what's REALLY going on and explain to you the ways you're actually doing okay, followed by the shifts you can make in order to get closer to what you actually want. Her advice has transformed not just my career, but my life and how happy I am in it, every day.

– Marsha Shandur,
Yes Yes Marsha

You're Not Lazy

Let go of what's holding you back
so you can enjoy a great life

Lara Wellman

Author: Wellman, Lara
Title: You're Not Lazy: Let go of what's holding you back so you
can enjoy a great life
ISBN: 978-1-7381244-0-4

Editors: Nicole Washburn, Darlene Turiff
Cover Design: Amanda Spencer, Onefish Creative
Book Layout: Eric Wellman
Photography Credit: Robin Andrew, Unposed

To order more copies or find out about other programs, visit
www.yourenotlazy.ca

To all of you who have spent way too many years of your life thinking you were lazy and sucked—turns out society taught us all the wrong things.

Also, to my kids Kiernan, Quinn, and Juliette. They're amazing and have taught me so much about myself and how to live my life.

Contents

Introduction

I feel like I never learned to "adult" the way I was led to believe I would. I thought by a certain age, I would be tidier, more responsible, not forget to pay bills, and not want to spend my days on leisure activities. Truly! I feel I was promised that by the time I reached adulthood, I wouldn't want to sleep in and that keeping the house tidy would kind of be like my hobby. **That definitely never happened.**

Instead, I'm *that* mom. The one with the lopsided bun held together with a pencil who doesn't think to check for stains on her shirt until after she's left the house. The middle-aged lady who has at least one coffee splotch somewhere on her person.

I'm the business owner who accidentally sent the wrong email to everyone on her list or inadvertently, or just uploaded the unedited version of her podcast.

I'm the friend who realizes that the perfect text I wrote in response to a message last week never actually got sent (or maybe I just crafted it in my head?!), so now I feel like an asshole.

I'm the person who just binged the entire season of the latest glassblowing, pottery making or sewing reality show instead of working on my extremely long to-do list like I'd promised myself I would.

I'm also someone who knows there are more things I could be doing, that I'm not as successful as I could be, and that most people have it more together than I do.

But here is the thing—everyone has stuff they aren't great at or haven't got to yet. Nobody gets to decide what "acting like an adult" looks like but us. This book is about reframing how you've learned to feel about yourself your whole life. This book is about finding confidence and trusting yourself. My big hope is that you'll see all that's possible for yourself because you will be quieting the self-doubt and self-loathing.

Society has taught us all to have unrealistic and unreasonable expectations of ourselves. We have inherited a faulty/limited version of what work and productivity should look like, and who deserves rest (and when). How we've been taught to think seems deliberately designed to make us feel crappy about ourselves, but we don't need to believe it anymore.

I want to normalize how many of us often feel, and help remind people that:

Everyone makes mistakes sometimes.

Everyone has imposter syndrome.

You have value even when you're not perfect.

I've learned that despite all my fears about not being good enough, I'm actually great at many things (and that has no relation to the state of my hair).

Owning that newfound confidence has significantly improved how I walk through the world and made me a happier/less anxious person! This confidence has not only helped me notice the good things in my life, but has also helped me stop dwelling on the ways I feel like a hot mess.

I've learned to stop expecting more of myself than even makes sense. Despite feeling like a lazy ass who might be pretty successful if I could just *get my act together and start living up to my potential*, I am capable of many great successes (and *have* been very successful.)

If you recognize yourself in any of this, or you're ready to stop feeling like crap about yourself all the time, you're in the right place. We're going to talk about being lazy. Actually, we'll talk about how you aren't lazy, but we'll get to that. We're going to talk about feeling like a hot mess, about what success looks like, and how to start redefining and reframing things in your life so you can stop feeling bad about yourself all the time.

Here's what I've learned from my years of working as a coach and the lived experience of someone figuring themselves out and finding ways to feel better in my own skin. Feeling emotionally exhausted and bad about yourself all the time is a big part of why you don't have the capacity to "get your shit together."

The amount of time that I used to spend feeling like a broken, lazy failure ate up so much of my energy and enthusiasm for life. Once I started believing I was capable, things shifted—and they can for you too.

I used to waste precious energy lost in the swirl of that mean voice in my head.

You know the one. The one that tells you how much you could be getting done if you'd just get your act together and how nothing is ever quite good enough. I was tormented by that voice, and yet what I thought was impossible has happened—I almost never hear it any more! I sleep better and fall asleep more easily. I get my work done faster and with more confidence. I also learned to confidently create and hold boundaries (and not even feel guilty about it!)

This book is about shifting how we see ourselves, re-imagining what it means to be successful, finding the energy to put towards the things we truly want, and starting to enjoy life more. Consider this your invitation to take many of the things I've learned from years of trial and error and self-discovery to see if you, too, can stop beating yourself up for being a lazy hot mess who can't get their shit together and start reframing all that is already true into a life that feels like success. It may seem like an impossible dream, but it's more possible than you think. This book is about sharing the ways you can get there too.

How to use this book

Some of the things we're about to talk about can bring up a lot of big feelings. As someone nearing 50, I have decades of feeling bad about myself under my belt as well as almost ten years of coaching business owners in various capacities. I've seen just how triggering some of these topics can be.

As you're reading this book, feelings of inadequacy, feelings of failure, feelings of regret or shame may very well rear their ugly heads. What I've come to learn is that it's okay to have all of those feelings. I encourage you to acknowledge and see and hear and feel them. And once you've let yourself do that, you get to start to figure out what comes next.

Without letting the big, scary, and hard feelings come through, it's hard to know what is and isn't working. These feelings help us know where we can adjust, and despite it being difficult, the information serves us well.

And so, if feelings like that start to pop up while reading this book—and I imagine they will—let them.

Don't try to stifle the feelings. Don't try to push them down or out. Let them tell you what's up. Permit them to be felt, and thank them for their service.

We don't always need to be okay. Accepting that and believing that is very powerful when figuring out how to step confidently into the next thing. And if all of this simply feels empowering or interesting, that's good too!

Who am I to be telling you all this stuff anyways?

First, I want to acknowledge my privilege as a cis white woman with solid financial safety provided by extended family and a spouse with a well-paying job. I know this colours how I travel through the world and don't pretend that it doesn't. I believe these ideas and concepts can help you break free of some of the rules ingrained in many of us. That said, I am always willing to and continuing to learn and grow.

I've struggled with anxiety, depression, and emotional regulation my whole life. I was lucky to have a family that never shied away from therapy and support. Despite so much support, I found my childhood tough. I hated school. My report cards from the time I was in early elementary school stated I "would do better if attended more often," accompanied with other helpful tips on how to keep a more organized desk, have less messy handwriting, and suggestions I try to live up to my potential. (Living up to potential, or feeling like you aren't living up to it, is a theme I personally have struggled with, and I know I'm not alone!)

Over the years, I've worked traditional jobs, but

I struggled to stay interested in them. I couldn't imagine staying in any one position for more than a few years (because *boring*).

I was never great at taking direction from bosses. I liked doing what I liked to do and simply froze during tasks I didn't want to do. I hated that bosses thought they could tell me what to do, even though I knew full well that was what they were supposed to be doing. From a young age I knew I wanted to run my own business. I didn't know what kind of business I wanted to run, but starting in my late teens I would spend hours dreaming up concepts. The very first business I spent hours contemplating was a meal planning and delivery service for seniors, which I imagined running with my mother (who is a dietician, nutritionist, and epidemiologist). I loved the idea of creating and implementing big ideas, and knew that having the flexibility of being my own boss would really suit me.

I started my entrepreneurial journey in 2007. My very first business was a clothing store that was dreamed into existence in the middle of the night while nursing my first baby. As with many of my business ideas, it was born from something I wanted but couldn't find. As I sat for countless hours in the dark with a baby who did not think sleeping without Mama was a reasonable option, I would get ideas. This was in the days before smartphones, so I would process thoughts from the day before. In this case, I was frustrated that I couldn't find any fun and clever baby clothing instead of cutesy

(*so* much cutesy!)

Since then, I've been a social media consultant, I've run a successful conference, and started blogs. Most recently, I got certified as a business coach and created the Biz Studio, supporting business owners as they build big things in their own unique ways.

The Biz Studio is the business I created as I started to embrace who I was truly. It was the business where I allowed myself to start doing things my way and to encourage my clients to do the same.

I know the frustration that comes from spinning your wheels in thick and deep mud and thinking you'll be stuck there forever. I know what it feels like to experience spaces that don't seem to work for the way you want to do things. I know bone-deep fatigue. I also know that it's possible to flip all that upside down and find a new way to think, feel, and be in the world.

That's what I want you to see too. Whether it be in your life, work, or business, I want you to see all the ways you can do things differently and start doing things your own way. And because I don't believe we're all the same, I have no one way of supporting my clients. We're always working to figure out what your best way of being is, what will work best for you, and leaning into that. That's what I hope you start to believe too. There's no magic solution that works for everyone, you get to go and find the right solution for *you*.

Things really started to change for me in the years since I turned 40. I finally figured out so much that I wish I'd known all my life. For one, that I wasn't lazy. That I'm not doomed to be an underachiever my whole life. That I legitimately struggle with things for legitimate reasons. Understanding this impacted both my personal and business lives and made things easier, happier, and less stressful.

Right around the time of my 40th birthday I received an ADHD diagnosis. I credit that diagnosis with a lot of the learning I've done to help me enjoy life more. This diagnosis freed me from the constant self-loathing and shame that came from feeling like I couldn't measure up to the ideals of the world, and it gave me permission to start thriving as the human I already was. I started to see my worth because I no longer invalidated my successes just because they looked different. By detaching myself from the shame of not being "enough," I started to acknowledge everything else that had been working well all along.

This book isn't just for folks with ADHD. My diagnosis and all the ways I've learned about brains and their differences since have helped me figure out how to support people where they're at and by working with their natural ways of being and doing. As a result, I have so much more compassion for how difficult it is to fit in and live up to the world's expectations, whether or not you are neurodivergent.

I'm writing this book because I want you to

see the possibilities, learn from my stories (and the stories people have shared with me) and start seeing the paths to success in front of you. I want you to stop beating yourself up for not being enough—because you *are* enough, just the way you are. Learning all of this for myself helped me feel so much calmer and aligned as a person. It helped me believe that I could go for bigger goals and create success, despite feeling like a hot mess some of the time. I genuinely want that for you too, and we'll walk through some of the simple things you can do to get there.

I'm also Canadian, so you'll notice all kinds of *u*'s where some of you might not be used to seeing them! Seems fitting for a book about getting more comfortable embracing YOU, right?

You're not lazy (really!)

There's a story I've told myself for as long as I can remember. It's a ridiculously simple story.

"I am lazy."

The End.

Short. Simple. And it came with proof.

I like to read trashy novels. (If you're a North-American Gen-Xer you might understand the pull of the uber-trashy worlds of V.C. Andrews and Danielle Steele books.)

> I binge-watch ALL the shows—from zombies to reality TV to the latest Netflix rom-coms.
>
> I often like to stay in PJs all day.
>
> I'm not always productive when I'm working. In fact, by my own definition, I'm almost never productive when I'm working.
>
> I don't get things done until the last minute.
>
> And you aren't invited to my house because it's always too messy.

This *clearly* describes a lazy person.

This story of lazy goes back to my childhood and university days too, where I skipped class and never did assignments until the last minute. I was very satisfied with a low attendance rate and solid C average.

I had fully internalized that I was a lazy person and would freely tell people that all the time. It was almost like a badge of honour. As if I was saying, "I'm lazy, and I'm proud of it, so you definitely can't call me out on not being more successful. I am *telling* you, and I like things this way!"

I would tell people how lazy I was, and people's responses wouldn't always align with the assertion.

> "Ummm, Lara... what about that conference for 150+ people you started and helped organize for four years?"

> "What about the parenting blog you started over ten years ago that is one of the most popular in Ottawa and that you've continued to run while starting other businesses?"

> "Speaking of businesses, what about the multiple businesses you've started?!"

> "What about the fact that you held down jobs and always got positive evaluations?"

None of it mattered because, in my mind, there was always more proof that I was a lazy person than anything else. That any productive thing I did was immediately negated by the fact that I like to watch a lot of TV and, some days, would rather not get out of bed at all. Compared to *actual* productive people, I wasn't coming close to measuring up.

Then, the year before I turned 40, one of my kids was assessed with Attention Deficit Hyperactive Disorder (ADHD). When you go through the assessment process for a child, you have to answer a lot of questionnaires about them. Over and over, as I answered questions about anxiety, avoidance, lack of attention to detail, and struggles with time management, I thought, "Oh, this sounds like me. Oh. OH! This sounds like me. Ummmmmm......"

When we went to the appointment to get the results, I started talking about how so many of the things the psychologist described related to me far more than just the kid we were talking about. The more we talked, the more I interjected about me and other family members—so much of what she was saying felt like our lives.

Then she said, "One of the most common things I hear from undiagnosed adults with ADHD is that they think of themselves as lazy."

My eyes bugged out of my head when she said that. To be honest, Lazy Lara felt called out.

I leaned forward and started in, *"Tell me more! I tell people I'm lazy all the time!"*

She explained that it is really common for adults with ADHD to feel like they are lazy because they have been conditioned over their lifetime to feel like they are never keeping up and they are never doing things the way they "should be done." Regardless of what they might be able to accomplish, they have been conditioned to believe they are never measuring up.

Society reinforces this constantly.

People who are not lazy work all the time. They hustle until they drop because that's what people who really want to be successful do.

You should want to be as productive as possible, and therefore you should work harder, sleep less, and stop watching TV.

We've been told productive people follow plans —they don't get caught up in overwhelm and go and take a nap instead of finishing that **very important project.**

We've been told people who are late are rude and lazy.

I have always really struggled with the "go go go" culture and take a lot of time to rest; I've been chronically tired, often due to actual medical reasons, so keeping up with the pace "expected" of me has never been something I felt I could accomplish. Because I was told everything in society is measured by how much I worked (and not whether I was reaching the goals I had set for myself), how could I think I was anything other than lazy?

Therefore, I spent a huge amount of my life and even more of my mental energy beating myself up for not being good enough, not being "grown up" enough, and not being "productive enough."

I'd created a long mental list of what I should or shouldn't be doing and decided I didn't measure up.

Deciding to own "lazy" took the pressure off. It created an atmosphere where I lowered people's expectations of me. I couldn't be disappointing myself when I had no expectations in the first place!

The truth is that it didn't take that much pressure off, but it became a mask I wore to hide the fact that I still cared that I didn't seem capable of living up to the world's expectations.

It gave me the out I always needed. "Look, here's the thing I did, but I didn't try my hardest, so if you don't think it's amazing, that's why." "Look, I know others put in more effort than I did, and I can tell you've noticed. So just know ahead of time, I wasn't *trying* to be as good as them—I already know I'm not."

It allowed me to claim mediocrity while also giving me many things to yell at myself for and feel shameful about. It was easier to take on a slacker mentality than to "own up" to not being able to keep up with what I thought should be expected of me. My mean inner voice would go to town, reminding me I was struggling.

"Stop wasting your time on mindless things!"

"Other adults can have their friends drop by their house without feeling embarrassed to let them in!"

"Other people don't have to talk themselves into getting their work done!"

My ADHD diagnosis allowed me to understand my brain better and recognize my tendency to be extremely hard on myself. It allowed me to look at my own behaviour and skill sets in a different way.

Once I did that, I acknowledged that when I want to be productive and sit down to do it, I am fast (that's the ADHD hyperfocus thing!)

I get things done.

I make things happen.

I'm really good at creating things.

I also realized that although I may be really fast, it takes a lot out of me. I can't do twice as much as someone else just because I can finish it in half the time.

Our society puts value on the number of hours we put into things and how hard we work, and not on the output (we're going to talk a lot more about that later too!). I believe it's time to stop putting so much value on the time we spend on things, but instead on the value we create.

Lazy people don't reach for the stars—they reach for the chips. Yummy, yummy chips!

The more I told myself and others I was lazy, the more I believed it and clearly even started leaning into it. I realized I had to start paying attention to that. By noticing that I was opting to believe the self-deprecating thoughts instead of what was actually true, I began to shift some of that thinking and stopped being so hard on myself.

The more I learned about ADHD, the more I realized that I had been conditioned to believe that

Stop putting so much focus on the **TIME SPENT ON THINGS** *instead of on the* **VALUE CREATED.**

how my brain works is wrong and never to focus on what makes it special and extraordinary.

It's taken me a few years to start accepting that I am a successful person who requires a lot of downtime to have the bandwidth, creativity, and motivation to do everything I do. I'm not being lazy. I'm properly nourishing my mind, body, and heart. I spend time creating art and connecting with people who inspire me, and I have the capacity to do my job better because I'm not as exhausted.

Could I do more sometimes? Maybe. But that doesn't take away from all the things I have done. Laying around doesn't mean everything I've already done stops counting. We must stop thinking that having a desire to rest means we're lazy.

Let me say that again more clearly:
RESTING ISN'T LAZY!

That's the story I used to constantly tell myself. It's the story I hear from my clients and friends. It's the story that makes it so hard to break out of molds, and do things differently. Honestly, it is such a pervasive message that you might be shocked if you paid attention to how many people called themselves lazy every time they did anything other than work.

I disassociated myself from the word lazy. You can too! Here's how I started reframing things for myself.

I'm not lazy. I'm smart not to burn out and push my body and brain harder than they're meant to go.

I'm not lazy. Look at that event I planned, that training I recorded, or all the people who are more active online this week because of a prompt I gave them.

I'm not lazy. I wrote a book!

I'm not lazy. I'm supporting my (3!) kids who also have ADHD and helping them have a better learning experience than I did, even if it meant homeschooling for a time while also running a business.

I'm not lazy. Sometimes, my ADHD makes it difficult for me to take action.

I'm not lazy. Many of my expectations of myself are unrealistic and unreasonable.

And you're not lazy, either. Whether you have ADHD or not—this applies to neurotypicals and neurodivergent alike. If any of this seems relatable, this book will give you many ways to start reframing how you look at life.

I will talk about how to uncover what you're REALLY good at and focus on. I'm going to share the ways we're holding ourselves back. I'm going to talk about the ways that we beat ourselves up.

I'm going to share how to create change (mindset and actionable tasks) so that we can escape the constant sense of "if only I were able to live up to my potential."

For me, letting go of lazy meant shifting my mindset. I stopped leaning into "lazy" and I started getting more done. Removing guilt from the equation means I enjoy my downtime more, and I use it less as a safety blanket and more like the gift of self-love that I deserve.

I'm launching even more workshops, programs, and events, landing even more clients, and making more money by focusing on what I'm good at.

Letting go of the idea that any time you're not working you're being lazy allows you to enjoy your downtime, and often you'll find you have even more energy to do other things.

Let that sink in. Instead of judging yourself and denying yourself essential self-care, allow yourself to refuel and enjoy your downtime. Resting even gives you the energy to get more done. It's time to stop owning the lazy title and realize lazy isn't even really a thing! Every time you catch yourself feeling like you're being "lazy," remember there is likely something else behind it. Fear. Uncertainty. Disinterest. Exhaustion. Malaise.

When you've decided that you're a lazy person who "never gets things done," you are so in the habit of thinking you're someone who doesn't get things done that you're blind to everything you *are* getting done. It's a trap! And I will show you how you can start to avoid those traps. Let me share an example.

*Work doesn't always
have to look*
LIKE WORK,
*but that doesn't make it
any less work.*

*Honour and acknowledge
it all; you might be*
**DOING MORE
THAN YOU
REALIZE!**

What if you're already doing more than you think?

As I stood in the shower one morning, I was thinking about this book and what I would write next. The words and concepts were being written and planned in my head, almost as if I was writing them at my desk.

I do this a lot. I do it with talks and workshops; I do it with content that I plan, and I do it when I need a plan of action for almost anything business or personal. I could be lying in bed with my eyes closed, walking, or rug hooking on the couch. Anyone else looking might think I'm not working at all.

And because it doesn't look like work, I never used to consider it work either. When I described my process to people, I would say that I was a master procrastinator and would simply get everything done at the 11th hour. Magically I could get it done really fast and still have it be excellent.

Why could I get it done fast? Because I had been doing a lot of the work in my head already! I wasn't just starting, even if that's what it looked like to other people. If 75% of the planning and writing was done in my head, was I actually "just starting?" No! And while everyone (including me) thought I was being "lazy," I wasn't. I was processing, and I was thinking.

If we only consider traditional ways of working —sitting at a desk and typing, doing manual work— as "actual" work, then we aren't acknowledging the truth.

Work doesn't just look like one thing. Resting can also be work.

To be clear, just resting for the sake of resting is also fine, but I want to make sure you are giving yourself credit for the work you are doing.

Here is another example: I used to tell everyone that I didn't work very much while spending hours a day managing online communities and engaging and supporting clients (and my potential clients) on social media.

If I was working while sitting on the couch on my phone, I never considered it to be work. Why? Because people think of social media as goofing off and wasting time—and besides, I was enjoying it. We don't get to count things we enjoy as work, right?

People tell me all the time that they like something so much they would do it for free, or that they feel guilty making money from it. This tells me just how ingrained it is to think that work has to suck for us to feel like we deserve to be paid

RESTING
can be work.

*Work can be
something you*
ENJOY.

for it.

When we don't acknowledge the work we're doing, we have lots of room to define ourselves as lazy. It's also how we end up feeling incredibly exhausted and not knowing why. It's because we aren't acknowledging that we're working far more than we're giving ourselves credit for.

It's time to reframe ways of thinking and start looking for all the positives. You're not lazy. You're amazing.

Reframe moment!

You're not lazy... you just haven't been allowing yourself to see all that you accomplish.

You're not lazy, you do things the way that works for you.

You're not lazy, because that's not even a thing.

You're not lazy—you deserve to rest and do more of the things you enjoy in life.

You're not lazy... you're awesome.

Reflection opportunity

Throughout the book I'll be sharing some questions you can spend some time reflecting or journaling on. Some people love journaling, and some people hate it. Some people get value out of it even if they hate it, and some people don't. Choose what feels right for you.

Are there ways that you're working but not letting yourself consider it work?

What have you been told/taught (directly or indirectly) about what it means to be a productive person in the world?

How has that impacted how you behave?

How has that impacted how you feel about yourself?

How can you start to embrace more rest and self-acceptance in your life?

When that mean voice of shame is getting you down

Not wanting to do a thing does not equal being lazy. But it feels that way a lot of the time. We so often feel that doing more is always the better choice that we forget that sometimes some things just don't need doing.

We get so tangled up in the shame of being unproductive that we fail to consider that we know more than we give ourselves credit for. By trusting ourselves more and releasing the shame so many of us carry around telling us that we aren't measuring up, we can start to truly thrive.

What is shame? Merriam-Webster defines it as a painful emotion caused by consciousness of guilt, shortcoming, or impropriety.

Let's talk a bit more about shame and how it may impact your life. If you're anything like me, it's running a lot of how you feel about yourself, and that impacts how you take action in the world.

Understanding this can make a huge difference in how successful you feel. That is what I want for you: to realize you're already doing just fine!

I've spent huge amounts of my life feeling bad

NOT
wanting to
DO SOMETHING
doesn't automatically
mean you're
LAZY.

about myself and the things I've done. I would lie in bed for hours at night thinking about all things I didn't do, said wrong, or wish I hadn't done.

That nagging voice has been busy throughout my life:

> Why can't I keep my house tidy the way others do?
>
> Why am I always late?
>
> Why does nobody else lose their phone and keys MULTIPLE times every day?
>
> How do other parents manage all the activities (and the admin involved) to keep everyone's lives organized?
>
> How do people do all the things they do when I can barely keep up?
>
> Why can't I just get it all together and be adulty like all the other grown-ups I see?

My friend Marsha Shandur* calls that voice the Beast. It is the voice that makes us feel terrible about ourselves and makes us believe that everyone else has it more together. It's a voice that we need to know is lying to us.

All these things are feelings of shame. They are exhausting and make you feel like a failure. One of my biggest goals in life is to help people start

---

* All the people I mention in this book are amazing and worth following. I will list all of them and how you can find them at the back of the book.

detaching themselves from that shame.

Shame is really at the root of it all. Shame is the thing that is holding us back. The thing that has us standing in our own way. The thing that makes us doubt ourselves. The thing that keeps us constantly trying to measure up even though we're pretty sure we never can.

It's such a big topic it needs its own book! For now, here is what I most want you to know:

Most of the time, the reasons you feel bad about yourself are unwarranted. They're due to years of trauma and internalized messages meant to make you feel bad about yourself. I hope you start to see how shame has been impacting you and how to let some of that shame fly away.

Feeling bad about yourself is exhausting.

Feeling bad about yourself means that you don't get to enjoy what you're doing. If you feel guilty sleeping in, watching mindless TV, or deciding to go for a walk instead of working, you lose out on the benefit of doing those things. Shame is heavy and depleting, and it's time to let some of it go. Letting go of the shame changed my life. The first step was understanding I had nothing to be shameful about.

Everything changed when I turned 40

Earlier, I mentioned my ADHD diagnosis. Here's why it was so significant to me.

Beyond making me feel lazy, ADHD shows up in my life and business in many ways.

It causes me to get distracted easily.

I don't complete things once they get boring.

I'm often really bad at detail-oriented tasks

There are many things I don't get to on my to-do list, even though I really want them done.

I struggle to keep my house clean, schedule appointments, complete school forms, renew prescriptions, and get updated passports.

I don't feel like deadlines are real until it's time to panic. (Not now... not now... not now... NOW!!)

I have a hard time gauging how long something will take. I'm almost always wrong despite accounting for more time to do something.

I was recently with some friends at the cottage, and we said we would leave to head back into the city by 11. When my friend started actively packing up just after 10 o'clock, I was confused—we had SO much time left; why was she starting to pack up so early? When at exactly 11, we started the car to leave, it became evident that my time optimism had struck again.

Being a time optimist means both that I always think I have more time than I do and that I am faster than I actually am. That time optimism translates into being late a lot, and every time I'm late I get really upset with myself.

As I started the process of getting diagnosed with ADHD, my psychiatrist suggested I read the book *Queen of Distraction* by Terry Matlen. That book alone made me feel seen and helped me accept that I wasn't some kind of anomaly. Other people struggled with the same kind of stuff I did! They too let food spoil in the fridge, seemed to always be running late, and never felt like they were on top of life.

Before my diagnosis, I felt a lot of shame about how I managed my life. The shame slowed me down, but even more significantly, I felt really shitty about myself. I would spend a lot of my time feeling guilty and shameful about all that I couldn't do that I was convinced I *should* be able to do. The mental load of all that shame was the most crippling part of life. It zapped my motivation to try to improve and change because I felt like I had already failed.

For me, that shame felt like exhaustion. The shame was the voice in my head that would go over everything I had done wrong that day as I tried to fall asleep. Then it would also start listing all the things I'd done wrong for the last 35 years. That shame would then translate into me being worried about all the things I wouldn't be able to handle in the future that hadn't even happened yet!

As soon as I started letting go of the idea that I was a lazy irresponsible person and embracing that I simply think and do things differently, the shame got lighter. I stopped beating myself up about everything and allowed myself to work with my brain instead of constantly fighting it.

> I started asking for help instead of getting overwhelmed and dropping balls.

> I started creating more realistic deadlines.

> I stopped feeling like a BAD PERSON when I made mistakes.

Embracing ADHD helped me stop focusing on what wasn't working and see my strengths.

ADHD also means I am used to trying new ways of doing things. I am creative and innovative. I am generally looking for novelty and change, which means I've tried a lot of things, and I have an increased tolerance for failure, because not everything I try works out. It means that I am almost always looking to see how to create more excitement and interest in life, and I am not tied to the idea that everything I do will work (it often doesn't). A little impulsivity mixed with creativity and lack of fear can turn into magic!

When I stopped focusing on all that I wasn't good at, I was able to start seeing what ADHD made me great at.

Jessica McCabe from *How to ADHD* wrote a song about how people with ADHD think differently and how it means that sometimes we just have to reframe how we're thinking. I believe this really applies to everyone because neurodivergence or not, we all have different brains and think differently.

It's simple: when things don't work out how we want them to she reminds us to "try different, try again." It's simple and yet so profound, and this message is truly the key to my life and how I coach people.

Over and over again, I talk to people with a plan of action that they're not implementing. Months and months of not doing the tasks they set out to do are only met with, "I *just* have to do it." But here's what I ask, "Do you? Why will just doing it work this time?" Often they are stuck in a shame spiral. It feels like the only way out of it involves doing what they're bad at. I suggest they find a new way that *will* work for them instead of believing the only way forward is through hell.

When you begin to let go of the societal expectations that surround you and make you feel bad about yourself, you can start thriving.

Instead of spending time avoiding things you

don't want to do, you start to find ways to do them that don't feel bad.

You start to acknowledge that maybe you'll be late sometimes but that you're doing your best. You ask people to remind you if it seems you're forgetting things instead of using systems that don't work and then getting upset.

You start looking for easier and simpler ways to do things instead of spending all your energy on feeling inadequate. You start being on the lookout for possibility instead of expecting failure.

The longer the shame rides along with you in life, the harder everything is and the worse you feel about yourself.

Later we will dig into some of the ways we feel shame and why. There are strategies you can start to implement to reframe what is happening in your life and start seeing things in a more positive light.

For now, give yourself permission to let go of the idea that there is just one way to find success.

Challenge:

When something isn't working, I challenge you to try a different way—what could you do instead to get you to the same goal? I bet there's a strategy or plan that's really great that could work.

Reframe moment!

You're not lazy because some things are difficult for you.

You're not lazy just because you don't want to do ALL THE THINGS.

You're not lazy for not wanting to do things that don't feel good to you.

You're not lazy for deciding you are going to have boundaries and opt out of certain activities.

You're not lazy for not doing things the same way as everyone else.

You're not lazy for opting out of hustle culture.

Reflection opportunity

How does shame play a role in how you feel about yourself?

What are some of the things you feel shame about?

What would it feel like to not carry around so much shame?

It's time to ask yourself "What if…"

So if you *aren't* a lazy disaster, what's going on?

Here's my theory: We are burdened by the lessons we've been taught throughout our lives and the shame attached to not measuring up to ideals. That burden means many of us don't know how to actually see what's working in our lives. Because we've been trained to feel bad for not being more productive, all we see is that we're failing at meeting (unrealistic) ideals.

I want to help you find ways to notice where you've been taught to believe something that isn't true and to start looking for what is true. I want you to start imagining what could be if you stopped feeling stuck in patterns meant to hold you back. I want you to be open to alternate ways of being or alternate ways of thinking and seeing what opportunities present themselves with that mindset shift. I want you to flip your fears of "what if it all goes wrong" to the more hopeful "what if it all goes right."

There's a special power in the words "what if." That power and the possibility that comes with it solidified itself for me at an event called Camp

Good Life Project.

For five years in a row, I attended a summer camp for adults in the Catskills of New York State. It was the closest thing I've ever experienced to living my *Dirty Dancing* resort dreams, but with people dressed in onesies!

It was a place where I could be around people who lifted me up. People who thought about the world the same way I did. People whose open hearts and optimism matched mine. People who run businesses the way I want to run my business—from the heart and with the intention to do good. The energy at camp was so positive I could feel it humming through my veins.

The people who went to this camp inspired me; every year, I would find myself taught by example to crack open my heart and mind just a little bit more, letting new ideas and feelings flow in. When I was there I could sense myself changing and growing more and more into the human I wanted to be. The human I was meant to be.

The camp experience included many of the same nostalgic pieces as camps for kids—arts and crafts (my favourite!), swimming in the lake, and of course, a talent show.

During my first year at camp, I sat in the talent show crowd and watched incredibly brave campers showcase a variety of talents (there was poetry, singing, improv, and one woman even did a stripping routine). My anxiety crept up my throat and made me cover my eyes with my hands to shield myself from what was happening on stage. I thought, "Now there is something I would never do!"

I am the kind of person who can't handle secondhand embarrassment—I will fast-forward through or go to the bathroom if someone in a show or movie scene is about to do something awkward.

That night my secondhand embarrassment was in overdrive, and I decided talent shows weren't for me; I snuck out and returned to my cabin early.

By year two of camp, my experience had shifted significantly. I'd had a big year with lots of personal growth and a new understanding of myself. That year as I watched the show I wasn't filled with secondhand embarrassment. Instead, I just felt awe. I watched people be vulnerable and creative. I didn't want to run away—I cried, laughed, and clapped until the end of the show.

I left feeling impressed and envious of those people's ability to share pieces of themselves like that. I was so grateful they dared to do it. Although I could never be that person, I knew the value of doing it was incredibly powerful.

In year three, the camp's founder, Jonathan Fields, kicked off camp with a challenge.

We were challenged to look for opportunities over the course of our three-and-a-half days at camp, and consider things we might have otherwise skipped. He suggested we ask ourselves, "What if...?" What if things could work out better than we thought? What if we were more capable than we believed?

In that moment, I decided to embrace the challenge and look for "What if" moments whenever I could. The talent show popped into my mind.

What if I took a baby step and offered to help with someone else's talent show act? The idea terrified me, but "What if it's worth doing anyway?". Over the next few days I spent a lot of time thinking about it, then actively shutting down the possibility. My inner critic had a lot to say about me, even while simply contemplating the idea.

> "You don't have a talent to share!"

> "More than enough people want to participate in the talent show. You don't need to be one of them."

So, in fear, I froze. I didn't offer to help anyone with their act.

Right before dinner on the night of the show, my friend Marsha and I were walking. She told me her plans to perform a call and repeat song from her days at summer camp as a child.

"I could never do that," I told her.

She shot me a look from the side of her eye and said "You say that like someone who would like to be able to do that, though."

gulp

"Maybe next year I could help someone with their routine," I countered. I envisioned myself as a cardboard tree in the background, quietly waving my arms around in the breeze.

"Actually... I could really use your help. I need someone to lead the audience in their response. You'd just have to copy what I do, after I do it."

"WHAT?!!"

I panicked. I could only imagine the look of horror that crossed my face in that moment. But instead of saying, "No," I brought myself back around to "What if...?".

> **What if** I said yes, even though I already decided being in the show wasn't a "this year goal"?

> **What if** I was brave and did a thing that pushed me out of my comfort zone?

> **What if** I let myself be open to possibilities?

I decided to say yes to Marsha. I wouldn't have a mic or be in charge of anything. I wouldn't be dancing or singing. The chances for embarrassment weren't all that high.

I spent the next two hours fretting. I was trying to memorize the complicated lines of the song and thinking, "What if I screw it up?! What if people think I'm bad at this?!"

I couldn't tell you what happened on stage before I got up there. I was so in my head about it all. Finally, the emcee called out our names.

"Next up, we have Marsha Shandur and Lara Wellman."

I got up on stage and I clapped and repeated my little heart out. And here's the shocking thing: It was not only "not terrible", it was actually also fun! As is often the case, the anticipation was the worst part.

I came off the stage on a high. I was beaming from ear to ear and there was a twinkle in my eye.

That night and the following day, people came up to me. They told me "You did a great job!" Someone even said "You were so charming up there!"

I fought every inclination to respond by diminishing my role or trying to make my being up there more insignificant than it was. It *was* significant. Taking the leap to do something that scared me was worth celebrating! What if doing the talent show was not only something I could do but something that I could be proud of?

What if getting up on that stage meant good things instead of scary things? What if it created growth, connection, bravery, and fun?

The talent show in that first year showed me my discomfort. In the second year, it showed me possibility. In year three, I let "What if I gave this a try" win, and it helped me remember there's even more possible for me that I don't even know about yet. In year four, I did what I thought I never would want to do. I got up on stage all on my own. I told the story of travelling through my fear of performing in the talent show, all while dressed in a lemur onesie! And it was amazing.

When I lead with the possibility that things could be different, I get to discover the version of me that's been hiding out and I get to know her more and more. I get to undo the years of conditioning and find the truer version of myself again. I get to peel back the fears and find my inner confidence.

What if I own my true power?

What if I believe I can go really big?

What if I can be that safe space for others?

I've committed to continuing the practice of "What ifs", because my favourite "What if" of all is simply **"What if it all works out?"**

I have proven to myself time and time again that by allowing myself to step into possibility and fear, I can grow and change more than I could have imagined.

You can do the same. Nothing is wrong with who you are right now, and discovering who that is and how to let yourself thrive is one of the best ways to find happiness and success in life. Simple as that.

Let's talk about a bunch of the other things I'd like to challenge you to think about when it comes to "What if...?"

Challenge:

Start looking for your own "What ifs."

What if success doesn't require misery?

Years ago, I read *The Big Leap* by Gay Hendricks. One of the many things I learned from it is that many of us fear success just as much as we fear failure. That seems counterintuitive, though. Why would people be afraid to succeed?

One of the reasons is because being successful feels really difficult. Society has taught us success requires sacrifice. It's going to be hard. It's going to hurt. That only the people who want something so bad that they're willing to go through hell to get there get to be really successful. It's simply not true.

If you have shied away from things that sound like they would be miserable, I don't blame you! We've been taught to wholly believe this is the only path to success. I certainly didn't feel like signing up for that!

This belief permeates every area of our lives. You might have heard quotes like, "Success requires sacrifice" or "It wouldn't be worth it if it wasn't hard." When we hear messages like that constantly, why wouldn't we think they were true?

Because of this programming, many of us unconsciously avoid starting to do things we think will be difficult. We talk ourselves out of thinking we even want those things.

We also tend only to see the extremes.

Option A is to work so hard you'll run the risk of burning out and hating your life, but since you'll be successful it'll be worth it! Option B is to not try, do nothing, and just be lazy and unsuccessful.

Instead, let's consider the option where there are infinite ways for you to choose to find happiness *and* success.

You can create the life you want (without hurting) by doing what works and not doing the things that don't work. Prioritizing what is most important to you, looking for easy ways to act, and making sure you have clear boundaries are the keys to success.

Here is what I believe:

Hustle culture is toxic.

Your best work won't come from a burnt-out version of you.

A tired mind is not a creative mind.

Not only have we been taught that hard work is the most impressive work, we've also been taught to think that things we enjoy aren't real work.

When we can start to detach value from how

much time or effort something took, we can start to see so much more potential for what is possible in our lives.

If you thought you could achieve something without sacrificing time with your family or money to do the comfortable things in life, what would you do? What would you consider going for that seems too hard to take on otherwise?

Capitalism has taught us that resting is lazy and hard work is amazing. If we stop glorifying hard, we can start enjoying our lives and work more.

What if you stopped believing pain and sacrifice were required to reach your goals? What would that mean for you?

What if you could get out of your own way?

In 2018 I was feeling frustrated in my business. Things were going well, but I felt like I was in a loop instead of moving forward. It was like there was something outside of my grasp that could open the doors to my business flourishing, but I didn't know what. What I did know was that I needed to figure out what that was and break out of my regular routines.

I decided to travel to Utah for a marketing/business conference. It was hosted by a woman who I followed online, who attracted the most fun and interesting people, and I wanted to soak in a bit of that! On the first night there was a VIP gathering, and I wandered in feeling excited but also nervous and awkward (because I'm not great at networking unless I'm the one running an event!)

I didn't know anyone in the room, so I grabbed some food, noticed a spot at a table, and sat down. One woman in particular had taken control of the conversation. She asked everyone individually what had brought them to the event.

"I'll tell her I'm here to get out of my own way!!" I thought. "I'll tell her I know I'm on the edge of success but know I need *something* different to get there." I spent everyone else's turn practicing what I would tell her. Finally, she turned to me, and I blurted, "I just need to figure out how to get out of my own way! I'm tired of saying something will change and then having it not change!"

I was specifically talking about my business here, but this was how I felt in many areas of my life. I would get stuck when it came to financial planning. Exercise. My social life!

She immediately started sharing stories about successful business owners who were more like me than the ones I usually heard about. She let me know that she knew what it felt like to be where I was. She shared strategies I felt could work for me and dispelled my fear that maybe I just wasn't cut out to be an entrepreneur. I felt heard and empowered.

That conversation was with Laura Wright, who became my coach for the next four years. I felt a connection to her not only because of how knowledgeable she was but because she made me feel more comfortable being me. She also was more like me than many of the other coaches I had ever talked to. She has the same big picture/big idea way of thinking, and wasn't process- and system-oriented like many of the other successful business owners I knew.

Laura and several other coaches held my hand (figuratively) as I started to recognize how to take action. I learned to stop trying to do things I didn't want to do and figure out what I *did* want to do.

I learned to create systems that made working with my motivation and desire for change easier without constantly starting over. I learned to recognize where fear and shame stopped me and when I was trying to do something I didn't want to do. I started to learn the art of self-compassion.

Getting in our own way is something a lot of us do. I see it in my coaching practice all the time (I even wrote a whole online course about it!).

Sometimes the reasons we aren't getting where we want in life are because we need mindset shifts more than new knowledge and strategies. Once we acknowledge that, we can allow ourselves to move forward confidently.

I see people regularly standing in their own way, and they're usually telling themselves:

I'm not good enough to do something.

I'm not organized enough.

Someone else is already doing it. Someone else would do it better.

Things need to be perfect.

Everything needs to feel aligned.

Everything needs to be figured out for me to be able to start.

I don't need to be successful.

I have to choose between success and happiness.

I can't do things the way they're supposed to be done.

I can't do something because I haven't seen anyone else do it before.

If you feel any of these things, here are some truths and reframes:

You ARE good enough; you've just been trying to measure up to the wrong thing.

You might not need to be all that organized (or you can hire someone who is!)

Whatever it is you want to teach: There are so many people who would most like to learn it from someone who can teach the way YOU teach.

Perfect isn't a thing.

Sometimes the only way to feel aligned and ready is to start.

It can feel easier to not try than to try and fail.

Success is NOT out of your reach.

Success and happiness CAN coexist.

There is no ONE way something is supposed to be done. You can change the rules.

YOU can be the trailblazer the world needs.

When you can start to recognize how you're standing in your own way by telling yourself things that aren't necessarily true, you can start to change your story.

What if you don't need to be someone else to be successful?

Do you ever find yourself thinking that there are things you'd like to do one day, but first, you need to reach some level of readiness or qualification? Maybe you tell people about all the things you have planned for your future and say things like:

> "I would really like to do that <big amazing thing>. I'll do it someday, when I am ready."

> "I would love to do that, but I'm just not the kind of person cut out to do that."

People spend so much time thinking they need to be "more."

That they need more credibility. More learning. More experience. More confidence. More time. More motivation. More charisma.

They think that who they are now isn't enough or that they are broken in a way that needs fixing to start doing great things.

They're convinced that they would need to

change for things to improve.

> I just need to stop wanting to watch trashy TV.

> I just need to stop messing around.

> I just need to stop being scared.

> I just need to DO IT!

What if, instead of having to change yourself or force yourself to do something you don't want to do (and that will make you miserable) you looked for a different solution-one that *does* work for you? What changes, then?

First, you're no longer operating out of shame that you've been doing something wrong or are not good enough. That is win #1!

Next, you start to see new possibilities:

> You watch trash TV because you love it. You don't feel guilty about it because you planned for that time and don't think of it as a waste.

> You figure out WHY you're "messing around" and adjust for it.

> You realize you were trying to do something you didn't actually want to do. Perhaps you were lacking in motivation, accountability, deadlines or enjoyment.

You can realize it's okay to be scared when doing big new things.

When you stop thinking you need to *be* different to find success, you can get out of your own way and start figuring out what *will* work. This is win #2—you get to start enjoying life more because you're not waiting for something to change before you get to do that!

You also need to ensure that what you're working towards is a definition of success that belongs to *you*.

What if success isn't what you thought it was?

Growing up, I had a very clear definition of success. It was created in my head based on the world I saw around me. It looked like this:

- Finishing high school and going to university to get a degree. And then a Master's degree. And then probably a PhD (My parents are both PhDs!).
- Getting a good job and moving up the ranks as high as possible and as quickly as possible.
- Buying a car and a house.
- Getting married.
- Having some kids.
- Buying a bigger car and bigger house.
- Getting promotions so I could keep making more money!
- Providing for my kids—sports, music, all the opportunities to make them well-rounded individuals.
- Keep going until the kids move out, I retire, and then I'm done!

I thought this definition was mine, but it wasn't. I never created it. It's what society told me I was *supposed* to want. The messages from school, TV, books, parents—everything led me to believe that this kind of success was what I was supposed to be working towards.

Don't get me wrong, it's not at all a bad picture. It's reasonably nice and I'm sure many people want and enjoy it. But here's the thing, many of us have a definition of success in our heads and we never take the time to check if it's actually our own definition of what we want.

I bought in and stuck to this path for quite a while.

I got a degree (I have a Bachelor of Arts in Psychology), and later, I got a diploma (I studied Public Relations in college). I travelled overseas teaching English in Korea for just shy of a year. I bought a car. I got a job in my field of communications. I got a promotion. I bought a house. I got married. I had a baby… and then I didn't want to go back to my job.

I started a business instead and quit my full-time permanent (with benefits) job.

WHAT?!

I jumped off my path—and I was okay.

I was okay with less money and "less success" because I wanted to be with my kid more. I wanted to feel less stressed and explore the life of being an entrepreneur.

I decided that my priorities weren't about success and that I was okay with that.

But now I see it wasn't that I didn't want success. I was just defining what that looked like for me.

My definition of success *was* quality time with my family. Success was not feeling stressed all the time. Success was making sure I had the flexibility in my life to try new projects and business ideas. And by that measure, I was successful! But I didn't see it that way.

As my kids got older and all three were in school full-time, my businesses changed. I became a marketing coach, and then a business coach, and money and career success came back to the forefront.

As an entrepreneur, a lot of what I saw in role models was to work all the time and *hustle* to build the biggest, fastest business possible. People out there were teaching things like "you'll sleep when you're dead" and "if you *really* want it, you're willing to sacrifice to get there!"

As the hustle bubbled back up inside of me, I noticed myself feeling like something was misaligned. Yet again, I needed to slow down and spend some time deciding what success was going to look like for me personally.

I wanted to work school bus hours. I wanted to take ten weeks off a year to spend many school holidays with my kids and still have time to do things for me and my husband. And I thought that meant that I needed to accept putting off success yet again.

What I've come to learn is that hustling harder isn't the only way to find success.

I wasn't putting off success; I was deciding what I truly wanted and prioritizing a life I would enjoy. Just like a good "choose your own adventure" book, there are many ways to travel through life and be successful!

And then the biggest surprise was learning that hustling wasn't the only way to achieve financial success. I was able to start finding ways to work less and still make money. While this can be easier for someone self-employed, there are also ways to think about looking for higher-paid part-time jobs instead of thinking you can't be making very much money at all. Or not getting stuck in the trap telling you the only way to do well in your career is to work more hours than you're contracted to fulfill.

It seems impossible, but it's not.

When I tell people I've made this shift in how I think about success, one of the questions I get asked the most often is, "But how did you make the shift?!" I get it, because it's one of those things with a flavour of "sounds great, but what am I supposed to do about it?"

Part of the answer is frustratingly annoying—it takes time and it takes practice. But more than that, it takes permission.

Permission to consider the alternative.

Permission to explore ideas and ways of being that weren't what you thought you wanted.

Permission to change your mind about how you thought you would want life to look.

Who gives you that permission? Ultimately it comes from within. Before I could start giving myself consent, I needed others to allow me to give myself permission first.

It might feel silly to need someone else to tell you it's okay to do something, but it's not. We all need to walk into new paths one step at a time and at the comfort level that works for us.

If you also need someone to give you permission, I'm happy to be that person. You have my permission to give yourself permission to change all the rules and do things in new and different ways.

What happens once you start to believe you have permission?

For me, it meant I allowed myself to pick my family over career success. I decided that making big money wasn't a priority for me, and was grateful for the privilege to choose that option.

Then I started doing more profound mindset work that allowed me to stop thinking the only way to make money was to work more hours.

I was blessed with the gift of not being willing to do all the things (remember how I said I leaned into lazy?) That's how I avoid being on the hustle bus. The work for me was believing I could still succeed despite that.

It may be like that for you too. Or you may be someone who suspects you aren't doing enough and feels badly about that.

For others yet, they feel so attached to being seen as productive and traditionally successful they can't see a path that feels acceptable witch doesn't include hustle. This is where you need to look within and ask yourself "Where are you getting stuck?"

Are you doing too much? Can you give yourself permission to do less and be okay with it? I meet so many people who never feel like they're doing enough despite working long hours. They're tired and they can't keep up. For some, the answer is to decide it's okay to not get everything done. To decide ahead of time that the measure of success will change and they will practice being okay with that until they start being okay with it.

Or are you sitting there thinking you're never going to amount to anything? Then you need to permit yourself to own that you're awesome even if you're not doing ALL THE THINGS. You're fully capable of creating success even if you don't want to measure up to what you think being successful looks like.

When you give yourself permission to dismiss what you thought was true about what success looks like, you open up to so much more possibility!

Let me introduce you to Marie Shinmoto. I've

been working with Marie for many years now, and when I first met her, she had a lot of stories about what work was meant to look like (hard, intense, and as much as possible). She also knew that what it was doing to her mental health and her physical body wasn't sustainable. The solution to improving her situation was one she had never considered.

I have been a physiotherapist for 34 years, and for the first 30 or so of those, I treated clients all day, every Monday to Friday. As I hit my 50s, this became harder on my body. By Friday morning, I didn't want to go to work anymore, not because I didn't enjoy my work, but because I was physically exhausted. But I kept doing it because, well, that's just how physiotherapists do it. It never occurred to me to do it any differently.

When Lara challenged my thinking on this, my first thought was that I couldn't bring in enough income working less than five days a week. It turns out I couldn't have been more wrong. I shortened my treatment sessions (I could actually achieve the same results in less time—guess there is an advantage to all that experience), which allowed me to fit more into each day, but kept my rates almost the same since the end result for the clients was still the same. I saw clients four days a week and spent less time treating, while preserving my income.

There were two big mental hurdles I had to get over to arrive here. One was charging almost the same amount for less time, then discovering the end result was the client feel better at the end of a session. Setting my fees for shorter sessions made me feel slightly nauseous, and imposter syndrome issues definitely came up. Who am I to charge that much for that length of time? The concept of paying for an outcome versus for a particular unit of time was a foreign one at first, but I now realize that because of my experience, I can get things done faster and after all, it is results the client is paying for.

The second hurdle was the thought that if I only saw patients four days a week I was somehow a slacker because REAL people work every day. Culturally, in my family hard work was revered. I never even heard of someone who worked part-time. So I felt that I was somehow less-than if I didn't see clients five days a week. I feared that people would give me the "well, it must be nice to have that luxury" look. Heck, I feared I would give myself that look. I may have once or twice! The worst of it is that I do in fact, work at least part of the day on Fridays on administrative tasks.

Clearly, this was an issue of outward appearance but also inner value. I had to come to realize that all of my needs matter. When I am personally fulfilled I am better able to meet the needs of the people around me. This makes me a better physiotherapist, a better business owner, a better parent, and a better person. I need a balanced life in order to have longevity in my career.

In the end, I realized that working harder for more hours wasn't the answer. It really came down to accepting the VALUE I had to offer and packaging it differently. I am so much happier and more fulfilled now that I spend less hours with clients, work less than 40 hours a week, and have more time to enjoy the great outdoors. Few things give me more joy than a 6:00 am paddle on a Friday morning. I can't imagine life any other way.

As a small business owner, Marie could only fit in everything she needed to do if she worked more than 5 days a week because she wasn't taking any time during her work week to be CEO. This might look a bit different if you work for someone else, but similar mindset shifts apply. If you find yourself stretched too thin and end up working evenings and weekends to try to get everything done, your shift is to start finding ways to stick to your work hours more regularly. Holding the boundaries of work from life can feel uncomfortable but often opens you up to having more energy and enthusiasm for your work again!

Sometimes, what's holding you back is feeling like there's no time or space. Sometimes it feels like you're not ready for change. But what if that isn't true?

What if you don't need to wait?

So, what if I told you that you don't need to wait to become someone different in order to be ready for the next things in your life?

In the early days of the pandemic I was invited to participate in an online panel discussion for a local charity. I've done a lot of these kinds of things and I was excited to take part. As the event drew closer, I was a bit intimidated (and a little excited) to find out the other panelists were a very prestigious mix that included academics and highly successful entrepreneurs.

As the event kicked off, I quickly noticed that all the speakers would answer their questions by citing research and statistics. I one hundred percent see the value in studies, research, and stats, but despite being raised by two academics I rarely use them to communicate my points. I instantly regretted not being that kind of person. As each person spoke and I waited for my turn to talk, I felt this increasing dread in the pit of my stomach. My inner voice was screaming, "The organizers made a huge mistake inviting you!!"

I couldn't exactly hop off the stage and shrink out of sight. So when it was my turn, I answered my questions the way I always do, with anecdotes from conversations I'd been having with clients and observations I'd been making about what I was witnessing. I was praying I could make it through the entire event without crying.

When the event ended, I sighed a huge breath of relief. I felt embarrassed, like I'd showed up to a formal ball dressed in a cat costume!

Then a friend (who I respect very much) reached out later that day. She said, "Thank goodness you were there! Your stories and perspective added balance to the event. If you hadn't been there, I bet people would have lost interest."

The voice in my head told me that in order to be qualified to be on this panel and bring value to the conversation I needed to be like everyone else. That voice was wrong. Being me with exactly the qualifications, insight, and experiences I had added to the event, regardless of whether or not I had a PhD. While stats and studies are useful, the other panelists had that part more than covered.

My friend was able to help me reframe how the entire day went. I no longer felt like a fraud. In fact, by being myself, I had done something helpful to create a well-balanced event.

Sometimes a party needs a cat, whether it's a costume party or not.

There are people out there who are looking for someone just like you at exactly the stage you are at now to talk to them. You don't need to be someone else.

WHAT IF
who you are right now
IS EXACTLY
the person people
NEED
to hear from?

What if you don't need to "just do" all the hard things?

Have you ever heard people say things like, "just believe it will be easy and it will be!"? That's toxic positivity.

What is toxic positivity? It's when people say things like, "Just think positive!" no matter how difficult the situation is. It suggests that we can simply *will* ease into existence.

This disregards privilege. Not everyone can change their lives for the better with nothing more than a mindset shift. Some people have bigger things to worry about: getting food on the table, surviving a nasty custody battle, or helping an ill loved one. It also tells people only positive feelings are allowed and they should disregard their true feelings. Telling someone to be positive can make them feel even worse about themselves.

This is another example of extremes. Not everything is either easy or hard. Not everything is perfect or garbage. Let's start looking for the options in the middle. Let's look for ease whenever possible!

I talk about this a lot because, whether you realize it or not, you've been trained to look for "hard". Both the protestant work ethic and living in a capitalist society have taught us that our worth is derived from how HARD we work. The messaging is everywhere; no wonder we believe it!

We believe so thoroughly that hard work is more valuable and better rewarded than resting or taking our time that we expect things to be hard. We forget that some things can simply be easy, and that's not a bad thing.

This means that even if you do see the easy option, you assume the harder option is better. This means you miss the opportunities for ease. One of the biggest problems with "hard" is that it's not a lot of fun. You might think it's the best option but if you're constantly trying to avoid it because you don't really want to do it, it's not actually better.

When you find yourself getting stuck and overwhelmed, you may start beating yourself up for being lazy. What if, instead, you look for a way to change the entire story?

Thinking the solution is to simply push through the misery is what's holding you back. What if you can reframe?

What if you can find ways to make the tasks more fun or simpler? What if you break them down into smaller tasks or ask someone for help?

Let's go through some examples of where you may be looking for hard and overlooking ease.

Asking for something

People get really uncomfortable making requests of others. It doesn't matter if it's for something personal or as part of their work. Let's take sending a request email. When they are ready to start writing the email to make the request, they start thinking, "I need to write an email that is compelling, includes *all* the info about my experience, the project, and what's "in it for them". This email needs to be *so* good, or they won't be interested. I only have one chance to get it right. I'll work on this later when I have a clear head and can really concentrate on getting it "just right!"

The pressure to get this email "right" has become huge. The desire to put off writing this email is now even bigger. The task list went from "send email" to requiring a lot of research, writing, and compelling calls to action.

Sending an email isn't always a simple task, even if we think it is. It will take a lot of time to do, especially to "do it right".

Not to mention, what if they don't respond?! Then it really will have been a waste of so much time! This task suddenly doesn't sit very high on the priority list when the likelihood of nothing at all coming of it seems high.

No wonder it all feels hard!

What if, instead of all of the above being necessary, you think to yourself that the first step is simply to reach out to someone with a simple message asking them if they'd like to have a conversation? (I get this might not work in all scenarios, but it can work in many, so stay with me.) What if it's actually easier for the person receiving the short message to respond to a simple question about talking later than it is for them to go through something long and detailed? What if this short message isn't "cheating" or "lazy"? Instead of critiquing yourself, wondering, "Why *wouldn't* I just write a proper message in the first place?" You get it done, send it, and discover that instead you're actually doing them a favour?

Ask yourself how to make things simple and give yourself a clear and easy-to-execute first step to move things forward. Doing this removes some of the dread that comes with a heavy task. The key is to simplify things, take things one step at a time, and accept an easier option.

Creating systems for work

Creating operational procedures for your work, like checklists, hiring processes, or setting up an email address for the new employee may seem like a thing you should do. Setting up these processes might have been on your to-do list or something someone has asked you to produce for months, but it never gets done because it feels so huge, overwhelming, and difficult.

What if instead of thinking of the operations manual as one task you break it down into smaller tasks? Record what you're doing as you're doing it (literally—screen record it!), ask your team members to write up what they've been doing, and review it. You can also keep a pen and notebook on your desk to jot down the order you do things as you do them.

Instead of thinking of this as a big, overwhelming project, break it down into pieces. This book began with a series of Facebook and blog posts I gathered into a document and tied together. It was still a big job, but creating it felt less daunting than staring at a blank page. When the big scary task feels too hard, ask yourself what a part of the project would look like, and start there!

Making meals

If cooking dinner is challenging for you (and you have the budget to pay for a solution) you could start using one of the food box companies. I often struggled with using meal kits because I knew it would be more expensive. It felt indulgent to pay for this service when I knew how to make most of the meals and I could get the ingredients on sale.

But the reality is that even if I go buy the ingredients, I may never make those meals. The number of times I've had to throw out carefully-selected ingredients that ended up rotting in my fridge is innumerable.

When I buy the meal kit boxes, something in my brain says, "Make the food." When I accept that this system works better for us, not only does less food go in the garbage, my family ends up eating healthier. By allowing myself to choose easy and not judge myself, things improved for our family.

Where else could you look for ease?

What about convincing your boss to assign you to that project you really want to work on? Ask! Don't wait for someone to notice that you're interested. Sometimes all it takes is to say, "I would love to do that." It doesn't always work, but sometimes it is *that* easy.

Our brain tends to try to protect us from things we believe could go wrong. How does it do that? Easy—by making things feel so scary we won't want to do them!

> "They're going to think I'm stupid."

> "I'm going to lose all my money!"

> "I'm going to have to live in my car."

> "Nobody will like me."

> "They're going to think I'm being rude/bold/conceited/pushy."

> "There's no way they would want to spend that money."

> "There is no way I am qualified enough to do that."

Some (most) of those things simply aren't true! I often see people catastrophizing things in my work, and I know that many of the thoughts people have are fears that aren't rooted in reality.

When you think to yourself **"IT CAN'T BE THAT EASY,"** *start responding* **"YES IT CAN!"**

Next time you're feeling like things are really tough, take some time to check in with yourself to see if you've been emotionally triggered or if you might be operating out of fear or old assumptions.

> Take a quiet moment to ground yourself and take some deep breaths.
>
> Spend some time checking the facts or doing the research to find out what is true. Sometimes looking at actual numbers, reading through some instructions, or finding out what qualifications are needed can help you realize things may not be as difficult as you think.
>
> Ask yourself if you might be stuck in a negative headspace and catastrophizing what the outcome might be.
>
> Ask yourself if you're slipping into old mindsets about your abilities or how things will go.
>
> Ask yourself if you're creating a story based more in fiction than fact.
>
> Check-in with a trusted friend or advisor and ask them what they think.
>
> Spend time checking in with yourself and consider if your feelings might not be true. This can help you reframe and move forward with more confidence and less worry.

First and foremost, here's what I hope you take away from this. The next time you think to yourself, "It can't be that easy, can it?" you realize that it absolutely can.

Then, whenever something works well and easily, write it down (or save an email). Things like a reminder—instead of a one-hour meeting—being enough to convince someone a project is worth them doing. Or the rave reviews you got for the event you put on (because you did a really great job!) These become proof things can be easy. Proof somehow feels tangible and more believable, so we use it when our confidence feels less stable.

Take some time to go back through this proof every now and then. It is so easy to forget, especially in the heat of a stressful moment.

What if it's not about arriving?

Do you ever find yourself thinking about all the things you'll do once you're more successful? Once you're more established? Once you're a little more credible?

Does it ever feel like you're waiting for everything to fall into place so that you don't feel stressed or scared all of the time?

These kinds of thoughts become huge hurdles on the road to feeling happy and content with your life and career.

What if you stopped waiting and just started?

The thought of doing that often makes me want to throw up. I don't like doing things I don't feel ready for! In fact, it's been a big hurdle regarding this book.

Over and over again, I thought "I have a book in me to write, but I haven't quite figured out what it is yet! I need to get it just right. I'm not ready yet."

Meanwhile, I could talk for days about all of the things I wanted people to know—about how they didn't have to wait to do the next big thing, about how it didn't have to be as hard as they thought. How they didn't need more qualifications or the money to build a custom website.

One of the most common things I tell the clients I work with is that they often put unnecessary roadblocks in front of themselves and could start *now* without waiting. Turns out I needed to hear the message again too.

I had to walk myself through these mindset hurdles many times while writing this book. Despite the stories and fear we're experiencing, the truth is: **Where we are now is of value, even if where we'll be later is different.**

I read Glennon Doyle's latest book, *Untamed*, when it first came out, and in it she talks about her two previous books. *Carry on, Warrior* and *Love Warrior* were both about things that stopped being true after they were published.

Her first book spoke of a happy marriage right before she found out her husband had been unfaithful. Her second book was about her marriage and surviving her husband being unfaithful, and by her third book, she had divorced her husband and married Abby Wambach.

In *Untamed*, she wrote about finding out about her husband's infidelity after writing her first book: "I was feeling the rage of a writer with a broken plot. Hell hath no fury like a memoirist whose husband just fucked up her story."

And when I read that, I recognized my fear. A

fear that what I write in this book could be wrong or stating things I won't believe five years from now. I was being held back by the fear of exactly what happened to her.

But Doyle's books were not invalid just because things changed. People learned from them and loved them. She wasn't wrong in the first books because things were different later. Internalizing that for myself was important and part of what allowed me to get my stories out.

Things change. We learn more. We adapt. That doesn't negate our previous value.

But it's so easy to think that it does! I imagine you may have felt that way at some point too.

Just because things might be different (and maybe even better) later, doesn't mean that what is true and real now isn't of value. They both are amazing, and the world deserves to have them.

What would you do now if you felt ready?

If you had all the right tools, certifications, credentials, and plan, all figured out... What would you do?

If you're waiting to feel ready, fully confident, fully trained and educated to feel successful... If you're waiting to be accepted, recognized as "at the top of your game," or anything else you think will help you feel ready before taking the leap into big things, I have some bad news for you:

You'll probably never feel like you've arrived

or fully ready and confident. The only exception is if you're ready to retire and make this thing your grand finale.

Many of us enjoy growing and stretching. We're looking for the next milestone in our careers, hobbies, and sports.

The place I'm at now in my business is so much further along than I ever imagined I would achieve when I first started 16 years ago. Do I feel fully confident and like I've finally arrived? No, because I have replaced my goals with new ones over the years.

When I get to the edge of my comfort zone in an area, I stretch and push myself into discomfort again. Not because I'm looking to create discomfort but because I know I love to keep growing as a person. It's how I went from being someone terrified of public speaking to someone who did some improv, to someone who signed up for a stand-up comedy class!

The same holds true for the art I make (I love making art!). I know many people who are the same way when it comes to sports, taking on new volunteer positions, and finding ways to help their communities. I regularly take new classes and try more complex projects, but that doesn't mean the art I made in the past is now worthless.

I am no longer looking to "arrive". I want to keep being interested, enthusiastic, and energized about my work.

This gets to be a reframe on "hard work." I

What is something you've been waiting to do until you FELT READY *that you can actually begin now?*

START THE THING!

know people tend to think that the hard work is the interesting work. Instead of thinking the next thing needs to be hard, I like to think it will be challenging.

I'm often looking for ways to stretch and innovate. I'm looking to problem solve and get comfortable with something I wasn't always comfortable with. For me, this is about growth, not pain, and that distinction is important. It allows me to decide with intention when and how to take on things that are challenging, without presuming it's out of my control and that pain is necessary.

So while I believe with all of my heart that we shouldn't be looking to make things hard on purpose and we should look for the easy way whenever possible, I also believe that we want to keep growing, which means there will be some discomfort along the way. Seven- and eight-figure business owners still experience fear, anxiety and imposter syndrome. And uncertainty doesn't stop managers and executives from setting new goals for themselves or their teams.

Stop waiting to arrive and ask yourself what the **right next step is for you**. Because (as cheesy as this might sound) when it comes to life and work, if we don't enjoy the journey, we are going to spend way too much of our lives waiting to feel good. You get to enjoy things now and not at just some far-off time in the future when you've "figured your shit out."

Reframe moment!

You're not lazy, you've been waiting to feel more ready.

You're not lazy, you didn't know you could start taking action even while feeling like a hot mess.

You're not lazy, you thought moving forward required sacrifice and pain.

You're not lazy, you thought you had to be someone you didn't want to be.

You're not lazy, you just needed permission to do things your way.

Reflection opportunity

If you thought you could achieve something without having to sacrifice time with your family or money to do the comfortable things in life, what would you do?

What if you stopped believing that the only way to reach your goals was too hard or painful to be worthwhile—what would that mean for you?

Are you standing in your own way? What are some of the things that you're doing that are stopping you from reaching your goals?

How can you reframe some of the ways you're holding yourself back into opportunities?

If you were to spend some time asking yourself what you would do now if you felt ready, what would you do? What are the "one-day" plans on your bucket list that don't need to wait?

The Rules are mostly BS

This is where I fall into a bit of my "down with the patriarchy, capitalism, and the old ways of thinking" rant.

We live in a society that is always about more.

More money. More productvity. More hustle.

As a result, there is always a call to work harder and do more. And to do it in a way that makes life simple for those in charge.

The way the world is set up does not best serve you.

It is set up to serve someone else: capitalists. During the industrial revolution, the factory owners decided the sun setting no longer meant an end to the work day! *Never let the machines sit unused!* These are the people who need us to work hard so they don't have to. It is set up to serve them—not you.

It's your job to figure out how to best serve *you*.

When you start to think about the rules of society as being there to support the people in charge so they have the easiest experience and make the most money instead of protecting us, you start to see why it can be worth questioning those rules.

The Hustle Harder/Girlboss movements in the last few decades have confused it even more. We've been sold the line that working hard serves us. That working hard proves our worth. You want to be the best you possible, right?!

The best version of ourselves is not the exhausted, overworked one who never gets to have a life.

Instead, let's question the rules! What actually *is* in your best interest? *Who* are you upsetting when you don't follow the rules? Are the rules benefitting you? You have the power to change more than you think.

When you spend some time thinking about what breaking (or changing) the rules to fit your own personal needs and goals could change for you, it can be pretty impressive.

We're going to spend some time exploring all of that, and at the end, you get to ask yourself which rules need changing and what new rules you're going to create for yourself.

It's time to get rid of
TOXIC
*messaging disguised
as empowerment.*

NO MORE:
*Hustle Culture!
Be a Girlboss!
Productivity at all costs!*

Breaking rules is good

I hate rules, but… I'm a rule follower.

As a people pleaser, I don't want people to be upset at me. That's honestly the biggest reason I follow the rules.

But it also means that I am regularly looking for ways to bend, avoid, change, or be in the spaces where I get to create the rules. I may not be willing to actively piss someone off, but that doesn't mean I will do things just because "that's how they've always been done."

Because I no longer believe the rules are unbendable (and I have had this attitude for quite a while) I've discovered many things.

- There are a lot of outdated societal rules that haven't changed because nobody thought to assess whether they need to change.
- Change doesn't happen unless someone is willing to say that it needs to happen.
- People don't like change.

I'm not suggesting you go out and start committing crimes! But there comes a time when even those of us who have been rule-followers our whole lives can start examining those rules.

Change can feel really hard. It means work. It can be complicated and it can be messy. That doesn't mean it isn't time to consider change.

Here are some examples of rules I think we can examine:

The key to productivity is working in the office

After the pandemic, some workplaces embraced remote work. Others moved to a hybrid model, yet others wanted their employees back in the office.

If you've had conversations about back-to-work, you may have heard stories about the insistence that going back to a physical office makes people more productive and connected.

They say that and then allow people to work in a variety of workspaces on different days. They may be working in offices but still have to connect remotely with their colleagues! They're now out of their comfortable in-home offices and being distracted in noisy spaces at hot-desks they don't usually use, not gaining any of the benefits in-person offices used to have. While some people justifiably need to be back in the office, and some people are happier in the office, others have been mandated back to the office for all the wrong reasons.

People who spent most of their careers working

*Remember,
rules are*
BENDABLE!

from the office might feel that it's the only way to do things. They might not think it's fair they had to commute into the office for 20, 30, 50 years and now the younger generation doesn't need to. Others again are worried about all the money that was spent to set up offices that are now sitting empty.

Change starts to feel overwhelming and uncomfortable, so they try to come back to what has always been. They dig in their heels and say that things are working just fine the way they always were. They prefer to stick with the status quo because that is the devil they know.

I don't believe all employees need to be in the office to be productive, but it has been the standard way of thinking for so long that it requires a massive mindset shift to change—one which not everyone is prepared to make.

It takes people standing up and saying, "We don't accept that truth anymore." for things to change.

School teaches kids the skills to be productive and employable adults

We expect that kids spend full days in school learning, regardless of how long it takes them to learn the information being taught. You'll often hear the justification for this as "teach kids a good work ethic so they are prepared for what it's like to work a full workweek as adults."

Our expectations of what school is meant to look like and why are so ingrained in us that we never stop to ask ourselves if we agree with them.

> What if none of that was true, and we're forcing old rules onto children for no actual good reason?

> What if rote memorization isn't the best way to learn something?

> What if questioning authority is something we should encourage in our children?

> What if aiming for perfect (A+) shouldn't always be the goal?

I believe that our education system needs a massive overhaul to actually serve our children well. That's another big shift in thinking for most.

There are so many things in life that we never question but probably deserve to be questioned.

Perhaps the person with the most seniority doesn't always have the answer.

Maybe writing a document formally isn't the best way to convey your credentials.

The list is endless. Instead of assuming what we've been told is true, ask yourself "What can change when things feel like they aren't working?"

Innovation doesn't happen by doing the same thing over and over again exactly the way someone else told you to do it. That means questioning the rules is a part of progress, not doing something wrong.

Let's dig in more into how we feel about rules.

We get stuck in the ways we are supposed to do things

Growing up, we all learned a lot of rules on how to be in life.

Be polite.

Be respectful.

Work hard.

The early bird gets the worm.

Straight-A students will have the best lives.

Follow the rules and be a good girl/boy.

Everything is a binary/black or white thing: sexuality, gender, lazy/productive, smart/not smart, academic/trades.

Many of those rules aren't true, but they've been reinforced our whole lives, so it only makes sense that we believe them on such an internal level that we don't even realize we're thinking them. And now they drive how we operate.

Because these rules are so programmed, they

make us feel wrong when we want to do things differently.

We think we "should" be doing so many things in a very specific way. The only "should" I actually recommend is that you shouldn't assume what you're told is true and that you ask yourself if you really believe those "shoulds" are the right and best things to do.

Trust me, I don't use the word "should" lightly.

I believe with great certainty that there is almost never only *one* way to do a thing. Most of us have very different ways of doing and processing that work for ourselves, and therefore suggesting that there is one way to be or do a thing is terrible. It makes most of us feel like failures and gives those in power more control.

I want us to stop thinking that way! When we accept that changing things means we get to thrive instead of it meaning we're failing, we begin to see the true potential that exists in the world. Notice when people explain rules with "that's how we've always done it."

Ask yourself if you could start using that information to do things differently. And most of all, remember that most people don't realize that everyone doesn't think like them, so they don't necessarily know that their system isn't the best one for you.

When you present other methods that come with clear reasons why these alternatives could be better, many people will start to listen.

Challenge:

Starting now, I challenge you to start noticing when the following thoughts pop up for you:

"This isn't the best way to do this!"

"If it were up to me I would do it like ____."

"I don't understand why they don't ____ instead of ____."

Just because you CAN do a thing doesn't mean you have to do a thing

The customer is always right, right?

Wrong.

We've been told we're supposed to always be doing everything in our power to keep potential clients (Or bosses. Or spouses. Friends. EVERYBODY.) happy, but that comes from a place of scarcity and control (theirs).

It presumes that you can't be successful without the goodwill of the potential customers to give you money. That you are meant to do whatever is needed to get people's money.

That you'll be fired if you don't do whatever your boss tells you to do.

That if you aren't trying to keep your spouse and friends as happy as possible at all times, they'll leave you/won't want to be friends with you anymore.

It presumes that there will be negative consequences if you ever push back on requests.

It's authoritarian and it's BS. It puts all the power

in your relationships into other people's hands and creates circumstances that make it feel like there is never an end to the work, and that you're never as appreciated as you could be.

You do not need to do all the things for all the people.

When we are clear on our boundaries, people know what to expect and how to behave.

When we are clear on our boundaries, we make sure that we aren't wasting energy on the wrong people.

When we are clear on our boundaries and hold them, we have enough capacity to do the things we really want to do. When we don't hold our boundaries we end up spending our time and energy on things that are more important to other people than ourselves.

The clearer we can be on what we expect, what we will and won't do and when we'll do it, the easier it is to avoid situations that can make us exceptionally unhappy.

I think we've all been taught that happiness is a luxury we don't all get to have. That's a myth. Not only do you deserve to be happy, but it's also better for everyone if you are! Unhappy people who are drained, irritated and exhausted are not the people doing the best work out there.

When we stop and evaluate whether we're being selfish or lazy or if we're being thoughtful and intentional in our lives, it starts to feel easier to create clear expectations and boundaries for our lives and work.

I know it's not always easy to establish these kinds of new habits and ways of doing and thinking about your life, but it *is* possible.

Figuring all of this out is how I got to a place where I started to say no to things I didn't want to do—even if I was good at them! One step at a time, I got there, and you can too!

Here's an example: In my past career, I was a communications specialist. I have many years of experience creating online content for myself and my businesses, and I'm really good at interviewing people. As a result, contracts to create corporate content for websites and internal publications (a lot of interviews) kept landing in my lap with no effort on my part. And they paid me well to do it.

But I hated it. I would procrastinate. I dreaded doing the work so much that I would spend 3 to 4 times the amount of time that made sense for what I was being paid. I kept saying yes because "you don't say no to money, right? You don't say no to people valuing your work and wanting to pay you for it. That would be ridiculous!"

But I didn't want to do the work. So I stopped accepting contracts doing that kind of work. Did I suddenly not have any money? No. Because saying no to the things I didn't want to do anymore (even when they pay well) benefitted me more than saying yes. Not only was I *not* doing work that I didn't want to do anymore, I had the time and energy to find opportunities I did enjoy. And that's exactly what happened.

I launched new programs. I ran more workshops. I let myself use my creativity to figure out what could come next.

When you are over capacity (both in actual time and mentally), you are no longer doing your best work. When you're over capacity, you don't have the energy to look for opportunities that you enjoy.

When you create space in your life and brain by saying no to the things that don't serve you, there is opportunity for new and better things to come in and take their place. I recognize this can be more difficult for some than others when it comes to work and the need to make an income. Sometimes the extra space can come from other areas of your life. You can make changes to how you spend and honour your time when it comes to your social life, keeping your home the way you want, and family commitments.

You don't have time to figure out how to improve things at work or at home when you're drowning. By saying no to some things you can start to get your head above water.

You also can say no to things just because you don't want to do them.

I went up to our family cottage up at the lake for a night with two friends. After I gave them the tour, showed them the view and my favourite relaxation spot, we settled in and started unpacking the groceries. My friends, who are both quite outdoorsy, proposed going for a walk. I didn't really want to go for a walk; for me, going up to the cottage is about sitting and relaxing until I've unwound. The area around the cottage isn't new and exciting for me to explore, so sitting on the covered porch enjoying the sound of the wind in the trees and the birds chirping seemed far more my speed at that moment than going for a walk. I'm honestly more about being nature-adjacent a lot of the time.

My inner critic had lots to say about that. "It would be healthy for you to go for a walk! These are your guests, you should spend time with them! You should take advantage of someone to get you out the door!"

But I just wanted to sit quietly on my own. One of the two friends had been to the cottage many times before and knew the lay of the land. So I wasn't abandoning them to the unknown.

I didn't go on the walk, and I got to enjoy my quiet, relaxing, introvert time under my favourite tree while they enjoyed their vigorous hike. Learning that I don't always need to say yes just because I think I *should* has given me so much more freedom to choose myself.

My old self would have worried that my friends would be hurt if I didn't want to spend time with them. This is a people-pleasing tendency. I know that my friends would have enjoyed my company. But I knew that at least one of them knew where they were going and were comfortable going without me. Regardless of whether or not they would have liked me to join them, they didn't *need*

YOU
get to decide what is
WORTH YOUR
TIME AND
ENERGY—
not other people.

me to join them.

I was lucky that the friends in question already understood what it means to have good boundaries and that my not going on the walk wasn't a personal slight on them. In fact, that night, the three of us ended up chatting about life expectations and how often we don't ask ourselves what we truly want and then let ourselves have what we truly want. We also discussed the importance of honouring our desires instead of worrying about what other people would want us to do.

If we'd been up for a few more days, I would have loved to go on some walks, but for now, I was happy to stay nature-adjacent and recharge my internal battery (Nobody was mad at me or judged me for it either!).

The weekend this happened, I shared this story on social media, and I got a fair amount of comments back from people saying they wished they could do that kind of thing (but felt they couldn't). I'm not going to lie, it takes practice. It can be uncomfortable in the beginning. Not everyone is always going to be as understanding as my friends were. It does get easier the more you do it though, and I think it's well worth the discomfort to get to a place in your life where you get to choose yourself first more often.

You get to decide what is worth your time and energy—not others.

If you were looking for a sign to stop doing something that you really don't enjoy (even if you're good at it or even if it's good for you) then this is it. Give yourself permission to stop doing things you don't want to do. If you're having a hard time giving yourself that permission, then I give you permission to give yourself permission. It will be well worth it, in the long run, to not be dragged down doing things you hate or don't want to do. I promise.

And here's another thing—it's okay to disappoint people sometimes. You don't always have to be the one to be disappointed. You may say no to something that someone would have really liked you to do, but someone being disappointed doesn't mean that you shouldn't have said no. You get to prioritize yourself. Someone being disappointed does not mean you made the wrong or selfish choice.

It's time to stop glorifying pain

No pain no gain—right? I see people say this all the time.

We've been so conditioned to think that pain is required that we don't question it. We think it means we're on the right track. We believe it makes us deserving. **We think things are meant to be hard to have any value.**

I once posted the following on my Facebook page "What if it was easy?"

80% of the replies that came back said:

"Then it wouldn't feel as satisfying."

"Then it would be boring."

"Then it would feel less impressive."

WHY?!

This expectation that we can only be rewarded after struggle is archaic and unnecessary. We can acknowledge that people overcoming adversity is a good thing without requiring adversity to make something good.

I want us to stop thinking that hard is required. To stop thinking the "rule" in life is that we are more impressive when we've done things that hurt.

That's not to say everything needs to be simple. It's certainly not to say everything needs to be boring. Instead we can think of something as challenging instead of hard.

I enjoy a good challenge. I do not enjoy hating everything about what I'm doing in order to deserve to receive the "payoff".

Writing this book has been challenging. Working on my mindset has been challenging.

In fact, I make it a habit to take on things that stretch me out of my comfort zone regularly. Getting on stage at the camp talent show was challenging, but it was the right growth push for me at the right time. I like to take on challenges, and I look forward to the outcome of getting to the other side of them.

I want to make it clear I'm not saying nothing will ever be hard or painful again. I'm saying that we shouldn't go *looking* for things to be hard.

As a business coach, I have a lot of conversations with clients who I see falling into the trap of thinking things need to be difficult.

Robin Whitford has been a client who also happens to also be my rug-hooking teacher (remember how I mentioned I love making art? I

We can
ACKNOWLEDGE
*that people overcoming
adversity is a*
GOOD THING
without
REQUIRING
*adversity to make
something good.*

love making rugs the most!). I asked her to share a bit about her journey and how her feelings around "hard work" have changed over the years.

I don't know how it happened or when it started, but I unconsciously and wholeheartedly believed that in order for me to be considered a good human, I had to work hard.

But more than that, my understanding of working hard was "blood, sweat or tears" (bonus points for all three!). Somehow I didn't apply this to other people, but the standards I set for myself to be considered worthy required extreme levels of self-sacrifice.

It took several years of therapy and a complete burnout (that took me years to recover from) for me to recognize that this belief was literally making me miserable and ultimately further from feeling like I was the "good human" I really desired to be.

I stayed at a job that was bringing me to tears almost daily and literally making me sick because I simultaneously believed that working hard equalled "being a good human."

The final straw was when I realized that doing what I thought I was supposed to do to be a "good human" kept me from being the kind of parent I wanted to be for my kids. Something had to give.

Luckily with an incredible patient psychologist and doctor, I learned there was still time to put on my oxygen mask and find other ways to be in the world. I started to change my beliefs about what it means to be human and understand what my personal values truly were.

This change didn't happen overnight and was not linear. It simply started by searching for alternatives. Looking inward, asking myself what I wanted, and looking outward to find examples of how others were doing things differently.

I started to read books, watch TED talks and eventually meet people who were doing things differently or "going to the beat of their own drummer" as some would say. I didn't look at them with judgement but rather with curiosity.

I admired them and saw that they, too were making contributions to make the world better without requiring "blood, sweat or tears" to define their worthiness.

It was actually quite the opposite. Having fun, spreading joy, being true to themselves, and recognizing their own needs, seemed to be their priorities. This was so inspirational for me, and it made me feel safe enough to explore this as a real possibility for myself too.

Ten years later, I have followed my childhood dream of making and teaching art and living in the country. I have designed my life around taking care of myself, being the kind of human and parent I always wanted to be, and creating a safe space for my students to explore who they really are and what fills them up. My new life prioritizes time sitting on my porch watching the wind blow and the sunset.

I run my business my way, and although my business model may not look like a typical model, it works for me and grows as I do. Of course, sometimes it's hard, and there are days when I may sweat, and there are tears from time to time, but those are no longer the criteria for feeling good about my worth. They're just part of being human and running a successful business.

I refuse to glorify pain. It gives society too much of an excuse to justify creating painful situations, and I've had enough. Don't let the world tell you things need to hurt. Go and look for ease. Pick the challenges you really want, and leave the rest behind.

How hard work can create a toxic workplace culture

"Hey, how's it going?"

"Good. Busy."

"Ah yes. Me too. Always so much to try to manage!"

It seems to be the script for most conversations lately. We live in a culture of busy. Everyone is not only over capacity, they worry that if they aren't busy, they will be seen as lazy.

The pandemic slowed everyone down, and there was a noticeable appreciation for being "not busy" but it has been very easy to slip back into old patterns. It's become so pervasive that we don't know how to not be busy anymore, and it impacts how we think about all aspects of our lives.

Now combine busy culture and hard work culture, and we've got some *really* negative implications for our work lives. A friend of mine often tells a story of just how toxic the culture of hard work can be.

Julie worked in an office where almost all of the employees worked overtime. They would arrive early and regularly stay late. Everybody would do this. Except for Julie.

Julie arrived and left on time unless there were exceptional circumstances. It was noticed. A meeting was called, and Julie's boss told her everyone else was willing to put in longer hours. Why wasn't she? Was she less committed?

Julie had a fast and simple answer. "Everyone is working overtime because they aren't completing their tasks during regular work hours. I am."

In this culture, the number of hours worked was valued the most, even though the work was always completed in a timely fashion. Julie even knew for a fact that many employees dragged out their work so that overtime was needed. They were playing a game to fulfill the boss's need for hard work in a way Julie wasn't willing to.

Still not understanding why Julie wasn't working overtime, her boss offered to give her more work.

When given the opportunity, this boss doubled down on the importance of more work above all else. In a culture like this, employees are expected to demonstrate their devotion. In many workplaces, it's become the norm to expect people to work beyond contracted hours for no extra pay (or even with pay) to prove their commitment to the organization.

We've been taught to revere hard work and to attach our value to the amount we work. The harder it is, the more impressive it is. The longer we work, the more impressive it is.

"They're so dedicated! They barely even sleep! It's so amazing!"

Ugh! Toxic bullshit is what that is!

We're trained to think that things are supposed to be hard and that we can't be okay with them being easy. We need to detach our worth from our time!

One day I got a private message from someone asking me if I might be able to give her some advice. "I think I'm doing something wrong," she told me. She then proceeded to tell me a bit about how things were going in her work and why she was confused. As she shared I realized that the problem she was having wasn't actually a problem. Things were going so well that she figured something must be wrong. Everyone else told her that what she was doing was supposed to be difficult. If it wasn't difficult for her, was she missing some important steps that would come to light later?

The advice I gave was simple: "Sounds like you're doing a great job. Keep doing what you're doing and enjoy."

That's what society has taught us—that if

something is easy, it must be wrong. If something is easy, you're tricking people, and somehow you're being sleazy.

I think it's time to realize just how harmful busy and hard work cultures are for us and embrace a "let it be easy" culture instead.

Let it be easy

I keep telling you things don't need to be hard, but how do you actually make a shift to finding what is easier?

First, you need to believe it's possible for things to be easier. If you don't believe it, you won't see it.

Secondly, you need to know that some things *are* hard, and that's okay too.

Our goal is not to suddenly think that everything we do is always easy, it's to be on the lookout for the easy options and to embrace them when we see them. When you start to believe it's possible you'll suddenly notice where your work doesn't need to be hard. You'll realize how there doesn't need to be a problem when things are going well. You'll see how value doesn't need to come from struggle.

When you believe that things can work well without them being difficult, you start to see new possibilities around you.

What if all you had to do to get a raise was ask?

What if your work plan is Post-it notes on the wall instead of a formal templated planning document?

What if letting a travel agent plan your trip lets you enjoy your vacation instead of being stressed and anxious the whole time?

What if getting something done faster than expected means you have some extra free time and not that you did something wrong?

What if you can reuse something you did for work before (a report, an email, a blog post) instead of starting over from scratch?

What if there's no problem with you bringing something store-bought to the potluck?

Take some time to look back at what's already working. What projects have you enjoyed the most? Ask to be doing more of those!

Think back to your best trips. What were your most successful family adventures? Go on more of those! Don't worry about what other people are doing or what you think the best family experiences *should* look like. Do what makes you and your family happy! All too often, I see people having huge battles with their families (me too!) to get them to try to enjoy something they really just aren't that into! If you can decrease the battles and increase the happiness, go for that!

How did you get your current clients? Do more of that!

If it's easier for you to have great family discussions while eating dinner in front of the TV instead of getting them to all sit at the table, then do that. One of the most common "parenting tips" I heard was to always have a meal together at the table. It is one of the things people most often share as the #1 non-negotiable item they're most proud of. It's their "thing I did well" item. Well, good for them. However, deciding not to do that does not mean you've done anything wrong!

People think, "it can't be that easy."

"I need to enrol my kids in competitive hockey and travel down south once a year," or "I must have to create a funnel, be on all the social channels, and revamp my website!!" or "Everyone else goes out, we can't just have quiet nights in all the time."

And maybe you'll do all of those things at some point. But if right now the simple thing appeals, do that. There is no one best way to do a thing, so pick the thing that works for you and do that. Don't go for what you think you "should" do, or the one you think sounds the most impressive.

Trust your instincts.

Trust what's working and do more of that.

Your friends won't like you any less if you invite them over for takeout instead of you cooking them a five-course dinner.

Finding faster ways to do things isn't cutting quality, it's finding efficiencies.

*Don't expect
things
to be*
HARD.

Everything doesn't need to be that hard all the time. Let what works flow for you. Let ease win.

Here are a few mantras to keep top of mind as you practice this:

- Easy isn't cheating
- I expect things to be easy

Challenge:

Next time you're faced with something difficult, ask yourself, "What would feel easy right now and like something I would want to do?"

Asking for help is powerful

Some of what we've been taught can be sneaky and insidious. One of the sneakiest is how we feel about asking for help.

Think about how often you've heard someone say, "You should ask for help when you need it! We want to help you."

Despite how often we're told to ask for help, many of us still struggle to ask. Why? Because while society tells you to ask for help, it simultaneously shows you how amazing people are who *didn't* need it.

> "Wow—did you see Sally do all that ALL ON HER OWN? So impressive!

> "Nobody even needed to show Kylan how to do this. Isn't that amazing?"

When people are revered for not needing help, we learn that we shouldn't ask for help if we want to be successful—regardless of having been told otherwise. The underlying message we've been shown is "Work hard. Struggle is expected. If you can't do it alone you're not as impressive."

It doesn't do us any favours that asking for help often feels like we're also losing control. Working in collaboration isn't something most of us feel comfortable with and we all have experienced or heard stories of team members not pulling their weight. It all works together to create the perfect situation for "it'll just be better if I figure this out on my own."

There is actually a lot of power in figuring out how to ask for help and learning to receive it when it arrives. So let's reframe some ideas around help.

Asking for help brings ease

Asking for help gives you shortcuts—and get this, shortcuts *aren't* cheating, especially in a world where we embrace ease.

Rather than attempting to forge your own path through the brush, you can get where you're going much faster with a guide who has taken the trip 1000 times before. Having a guide show you the way isn't cheating, it's exactly what people say when they tell you to "work smarter, not harder."

Think of it as the way to avoid using a machete to clear out the brush to get where you're going. Instead of taking ten times longer, why not choose the cleared path 20 feet to your left? The easier way often goes unnoticed. Just because you know how to use a machete doesn't mean you need to use it every time you try to go somewhere!

Asking for help, advice, and support allows you to create the same output in a fraction of the time with a fraction of the effort.

"But then I won't get all the credit!"

I recently found myself falling into this trap while working on a piece of art. Something wasn't quite working for me, and I wanted input from other artists.

I worried that if I asked for help and got advice from others, I could no longer consider myself the piece's designer. But that's not how things work! Asking for help doesn't somehow make me no longer the artist. I get to decide what advice I take or don't take, and how to execute it. I'm still the one who created the design in the first place!

Asking for help didn't make the piece any less mine. I asked for advice, took *some* of the suggestions, and felt much happier with the whole thing.

Why do we feel comfortable asking for help some times over others?

There are times when we think asking for help is okay.

People don't feel guilty getting an editor to review copy; books get revised multiple times by multiple people, but nobody questions whether the author is still the author! The director of a movie is still the director, even if someone else is in the editing room making big decisions about the flow of the movie. We need to take that same mindset and apply it more broadly. If we remember that asking for help doesn't take away anything from our value, we can allow ourselves to be helped and supported more often.

Someone giving you a map doesn't erase/diminish the significance of your achievement on that trek. You were trying to get somewhere, not taking part in a "find the route" competition. And you *did* get there, celebrate that fact!

Collaboration helps us all

We're often stronger when we work together. While some people think it's less impressive if you got help, we can change that narrative. Be a trailblazer with me and let's say no to toxic thinking.

Reframe moment!

You're not lazy, you have boundaries.

You're not lazy when you ask for help.

You're not lazy when you would rather look for the easy way instead of the hard way.

You're not lazy when you don't want to do things you don't enjoy or work with people you don't like.

You're not lazy, you're using other people's expertise so you don't have to re-invent the wheel.

Reflection opportunity

What would you do if you weren't worried about someone (and that someone could be you!) thinking you were being lazy?

What are some of the reasons you avoid asking for help?

What are some things that, going forward, you'll ask for support with?

Failure isn't bad.
Perfect isn't
the goal.

We don't want to be bad at things. Seems obvious. But should it be?

Why is being bad at something considered so terrible? It's because we're taught that being bad at something means failure, and we're taught to feel shame when it comes to our failures.

From our earliest days in school, we are encouraged to get the highest grades possible and are berated for low grades. We're also taught there is a right way and a wrong way. We need to know the "right" way, or else people will be disappointed in us. It's a LOT of pressure!

I want to reframe how we look at failure.

First, we must remember that we're not supposed to be good at something the first time we try it. It takes time and practice to hone a skill. Actors practise their lines for months before they actually begin filming or get on stage. Writers have many revisions before a manuscript is ready for publishing. You start with addition before you tackle algebra.

I get it. I don't like not being great at something

right from the start either. The thing is, the need for "more!" "better!" "faster!" has created unrealistic expectations of perfection that now set us up for failure. Making sure we remember it's not typical to get things right the first time is important. We aren't failing at anything; we are actively doing the things required to do to get better at something.

Trying things and having them not work may feel like failure, but if we were in a laboratory we wouldn't feel that way! Like I said before, innovation comes from a willingness to try new things, knowing that they very well might not work.

If we can begin thinking of the things we try as "experiments" and not "surefire", we don't need to be so hard on ourselves if they don't work the first time.

Would that change how you feel about the things you do? What if you thought "People won't judge me if it doesn't work. In fact, they'll love that I try new things, and that I'm searching for what *does* work"? Would that take some of the pressure off?

When you look up failure in multiple dictionaries, you'll see the same themes repeatedly. "Lack of success," "falling short," "the act of not doing something you were expected to do." There it is again: "did not measure up"—which sounds like, "not as good as you could have been, you slacker!" No wonder we try to avoid it at all costs!

When we notice how terrified we are of being

seen as failures, we realize our expectations are skewing reality and some things we think of as failures are not failures at all! When you accept that not being good at something right off the bat doesn't mean you're bad at it, you can embrace the discomfort of "failure" and use it to your advantage.

You're not failing; you're learning.

Perfect isn't the goal

What is perfect anyways? And why are we so intent on achieving it?

Just as we're taught to fear failure, we're taught to always strive for perfection. But here's the thing I've learned—there's no perfect.

If you're reading this and are feeling a bit skeptical when I tell you that, I get it. What I truly mean is, "There is no universal perfect." What is perfect to you is not perfect to someone else. To one person, big is perfect. To another, small is perfect. For some, minimalism is the perfect aesthetic; for others, maximalism is. We can't always please everyone, but trying to can become exhausting and demoralizing.

When we realize this almighty perfection isn't possible, we can release ourselves from the goal of striving for it. We get to decide what is right for us. We get to let go of the expectation that we could ever do something that would make everyone happy. Trying to live up to all of this perfection is exhausting! No wonder we freeze up and then call ourselves lazy!

Want more examples?

Many years ago, I ran a social media conference called Social Capital. It ran for four years, attracting hundreds of people and big-name sponsors. After every event, we would send out a survey to attendees to find out what they thought. Without fail, we would get answers like:

- "This was the best food I've ever had at a conference!"
- "This is the worst food I've ever tasted. It went straight in the garbage!"
- "The content was too basic; I didn't learn anything."
- "The content was too advanced; I felt it was over my head."
- "The ticket prices were outrageous. For that price, I would expect bigger names than you had."
- "I run events for a living. You're not charging enough for this event—you must be barely breaking even." (This was true, by the way. We basically ran this conference as volunteers!)

No matter what we did, there seemed to be someone who thought it was more than they ever expected and someone who thought it was below average. That experience taught me to let go of the expectation that there was anything that could please anyone, and it was liberating!

Let go of the people pleasing! Let go of aiming

for perfection! Let go of the pressure we create that really isn't necessary.

Is there a perfect Christmas tree?

My perfect Christmas tree is full of ornaments from my childhood, made by my children in kindergarten, and from special moments throughout my life. We look for an ornament on every trip we take to add to our tree. Every year I spend hours going through the memories held in the tree.

This is a very different experience for the person who holds immense pleasure in curating a aesthetically pleasing tree or for the person who is happy to have a small ceramic tree on their side table to celebrate without the work needed to put up and decorate. All options are perfect for the people who choose them to be so. No option suits everyone perfectly.

Is there a perfect family?

My whole life, I knew I wanted to have children. When I was in my mid-twenties, my biological clock (or maybe just societal expectations) sounded a ten-alarm blaze screaming "You're getting too old for babies!!" Before meeting my husband, I had concocted plans for taking on the challenge of parenting solo. For me, children felt like the correct answer. Luckily, I met a great guy on a similar timeline as me and, by the age of 32, I was married, owned a house and had three children under three (thanks to the arrival of twins during my second pregnancy.)

Not everyone wants to have children. Not everyone even wants to get married or have a partner at all. Some people want multiple partners. Some people create communities of families together so they can support one another.

All of these options are imperfect for some and perfect for others. I should no more try to convince people that getting married, living in the suburbs, and having children is the correct answer for them, than they should try to convince me that I should never have had children in the first place. But people do that. We believe there are right ways and wrong ways. Perfect ways and failures. It's simply not true.

Is there a perfect strategy for work?

Some people believe the perfect strategy for planning a big project is a 50-page document with accompanying details and fully set up project management software for the team. They thrive on a solid plan and update it daily to feel motivated and like they're staying on track.

For me, a big-picture plan highlighted on a whiteboard with high-level benchmarks feels easier to create and follow through on. I won't remember to log in and check the tasks in a project planning software, so why bother setting it all up?

Neither is a wrong choice; neither is everyone's version of perfect.

When we understand that there is no perfect

or "best" solution, we have the freedom to intentionally make better choices for ourselves.

This is what I hope we can all do more of in our lives. Clear out the "I should do it *this* way for people to find it valuable." Instead ask yourselves what will work best for the way your brains work, for the capacity you have, for the people that will be impacted by it, by your motivation, and by the actual goals.

When we aim for perfection, we often get so bogged down that we freeze and don't produce anything at all.

Perhaps you truly believe there is more value in the "perfect" version of something you'd like to create, but there is no value if nothing ever gets created.

You're probably already convinced, but here's another example of how aiming for perfection gets us stuck:

The first course I launched looked nothing like the one I thought I would create.

Way back in 2012, I took a popular online course for business owners called BSchool. I had a business partner then, and we dreamed of having our own online portal and course called Social Media Simplified that was of the same calibre and style as BSchool.

What we weren't taking into account was that the course's creator, Marie Forleo, has a much bigger team and budget than we did. Back then, there were no easy tools to build an online course.

Creating something similar to BSchool required a graphic designer and someone to code a website for us. The time and financial investment necessary to build something like that was huge. We spent thousands of dollars and still didn't have a course; it was just too big a project for our capacity.

After a couple of years of *not* getting this course out into the world (and amicably dissolving my partnership with my business partner), I finally launched my first course. I trashed the whole Forleo-style program, and sold a 5-week program for under $100, delivered entirely by email.

The first course would have been good and potentially amazing and more impressive. But it had a huge disadvantage: *it did not exist* and never was going to. Instead, the simpler version did its job really well. And I didn't break the bank to build it!

Take a moment now. Ask yourself if there is anything you could be avoiding because doing it the way you "should" feels too hard. Could it potentially be done a different way?

Instead of picking between "perfect" and "never done," give yourself the gift of taking the simple option sometimes. Step away from all the feelings you have around, "This is hard," and look for ways to make it easier. What if it was easy?

Remember that there is no perfect. Let go of that unachievable goal and start experiencing different ways of being.

Stop thinking you'll ever
get it all done

I know that the title of this chapter sounds discouraging, but stay with me, and you'll see how it's not.

Just like we shouldn't focus on arriving, we don't want to get stuck thinking we only achieve success when our to-do lists are complete. By never being satisfied until everything is done, we set ourselves up to never be satisfied.

Here's the thing: There are always new things to add to our lists, because life and work keep evolving and moving.

The more time available, the more ways we fill it. Instead of thinking our goal is to fully complete everything on our list, start expecting it to be a living document. You're not meant to have no list left.

You're not failing!

Here is what I see all the time.

We have a long and ambitious to-do list. First, we believe everything on that list will take at least half the time it will actually take (there's that time optimism again!) and despite our best intentions we know it's too much to get done in a reasonable time frame.

Then add the fact that we are constantly pushed to think we need to get as much done as possible *all of the time*. This makes everything feel "URGENT" and "LATE", meaning we're always behind. Again, shame is coming in to tell us we are failures.

"You're always behind. You can't keep up. You're not good enough!!"

It doesn't matter if the goals were unrealistic. Not meeting our unrealistic goals makes us feel like failures and stops us from being able to see our accomplishments.

We get so bogged down in what we haven't accomplished that we never stop and celebrate what has gone well and what we're good at.

There's an exercise I take many of my clients through where I ask them to list all their wins from a 3-, 6-, or 12-month period. I ask them to spend ten minutes writing down everything they can think of (some of them use their calendars to help them remember). At the end, people are almost always surprised because they got so much more done than they had remembered. Once they stop and look is really shocking to most, in a good way.

Instead of feeling like someone who never gets things done (I mean—good grief, look at the size of their to-do lists!), they see proof that they've been getting stuff done all along.

They remember the project they worked on for six months being met with accolades, even though, at the time, they had to move on to the next project without even thinking about celebrating.

They realize they completed several projects around the house and that they are already enjoying the results, even though at the time they just went on to fretting about the other projects they needed to start.

They celebrate the boundaries they set to protect their time and energy.

And countless more examples.

When you spend life feeling like there's always more to do and you're always behind, you live in a state of anxiety and stress. When you can alleviate some of the urgency and heaviness around what still needs to come and celebrate your accomplishments, you change how your days feel. It's not about getting it all done; it's about understanding your priorities, celebrating your ability to do things, and giving yourself some grace when it comes to how much pressure you feel all of the time. Don't expect more than 2–3 items to be knocked off your list daily. When you're more realistic and purposeful, you feel more aligned with your goals instead of just doing everything for the sake of doing them.

Cut yourself some slack when you see how much "more" there is to do and celebrate the opportunity to face new challenges, and prioritize what you're going to work on next.

Challenge:

Spend a few minutes listing all your wins from the last six months (personal and work). Then take some time to not only notice all you've accomplished but also to celebrate it.

Not everything on your to-do list actually needs to get done

We've already talked about the culture of busy and how we shouldn't expect to get everything done all of the time. But despite knowing all that, we still have a long to-do list constantly staring us in the face.

What if it's because you're doing more than you need to?

What would happen if you started saying "no" a bit more often?

Unrealistic expectations for what can be done come from both outside and inside of us. The pressure to get everything done feels so real, but there are opportunities to say no to some things.

Here are some things to consider as you examine your to-do list so we can clear it out and find more time and space for you. We're going to talk about the three Ds: delete, defer and delegate.

Delete

Ask yourself, "Do I actually need to do that

thing, or do I just think I need to do it? What can I **delete** from my list?"

What kinds of things could you start saying no to? It could be things like sending Christmas cards or always baking a treat when your kids have friends over. These might be things that you like to do but that have become a burden because there is never enough time.

There may also be things you're saying yes to that you never wanted to say yes to in the first place. It's okay to start saying no if you don't have the capacity or desire to do certain things. This is true at work, with friends and family, or even in volunteer positions.

Defer

Ask yourself, "Are the items on my list priorities? Are they helping me achieve my goals, or are they nice to have things that don't have an actual deadline?"

It may be time to **defer** them and stop letting them hang over your head for a while.

Examples can include everything from "reorganize the linen closet" because although that would be nice, it's not important enough to prioritize or create new systems for your workplace. Do they need to happen soon? Or can you actively decide they aren't a "now thing"? If so, then you can stop feeling guilty every time you see it on your list, knowing it won't get done.

Delegate

Now look at the rest of the list and ask yourself "Is there someone else who I could **delegate** these tasks to?" A family member, a staff member? Should you hire someone to paint the family room or write that email sequence? Not everything needs to be done by you. Asking someone else to help, or paying someone (if you have the budget), can immensely ease your workload and mind.

There are always things you can stop doing or find ways to do more effectively. Most of us get so busy just *doing* that we don't stop to ensure we're doing the right things and using our time well.

As a business coach I've read quite a lot about how to be more productive (and make more money!) in business. One of the most interesting tools I learned about is the Eisenhower matrix and it applies to all parts of life!

This is a tool that has been used by many and adapted by many others. Regardless of who is using it, the basics remain the same.

Your to-do list is divided into four quadrants, labeled important/not important tasks versus urgent/not urgent tasks.

We (most human adults) spend most of our time focusing on things that are urgent and not important, or we get distracted with things that are not important and not urgent.

The quadrant that has a lot of the juiciest stuff that can make the biggest difference in your life and business is one we often put off the most: the important but not urgent quadrant.

We don't focus on those tasks because they aren't urgent. We know they're important so plan to get to them "eventually" but they're often a bit more challenging, and so we don't.

We have tasks on our lists with urgent deadlines that aren't helping us achieve our goals. These are some of the things we can start saying no to. We then get to prioritize spending time on the important not urgent stuff and find ourselves feeling a lot better about what we're getting done.

This is about learning to not just follow the "THIS NEEDS TO GET DONE!!" list. It's about slowing down and asking ourselves why we are prioritizing things on our list.

This is where we can start deciding not to do certain tasks anymore. To make really thoughtful decisions on how we're spending our time.

Like what, Lara? Give me examples of these meaningful important but not urgent tasks.

Reorganizing the kitchen cupboards isn't urgent. But it may mean that when you're in the kitchen you're less frustrated and cooking meals takes less time. This could help you increase your enjoyment of tasks that you want to keep doing or save you time to spend on other things that bring you enjoyment. IMPORTANT. Not urgent.

Having that difficult conversation with your boss isn't urgent (you've been frustrated for a year already!), but it could result in changes that make working more pleasant (plus you'll spend less time surfing the web for jobs you could apply to instead. **IMPORTANT**. Not urgent (this one feels like it should be urgent, but anything without a deadline easily falls into this category).

Okay, but what qualifies as urgent but not important?

Things that are about other people's goals instead of not yours. Your boss or a client rushing you on something that doesn't need to be rushed. Things someone else could do. These are the items that most often fall into the delegate it category!

When you slow down and really assess what is on the never ending to-do list, you have an opportunity to make changes that can potentially decrease your workload and anxiety, and free up time for the things that are really important to you.

Take the time to breathe and figure out what you're trying to get done and why. Then prioritize and decide what can wait, what can be deleted off the list and what can be outsourced.

When we commit to finding more time and minimizing the need to hustle harder all the time, life feels a lot easier.

Challenge:

Spend some time with your to-do list and ask yourself:

- What are you doing that's urgent but not important? Start doing less of those. Delegate or delete!!

- What is taking up a lot of your time but not getting results? Make a list. Can you skip it for a day or a week? Can you just stop doing it?

- What takes you a long time because you hate doing it or you're not very good at it?

- What could you spend just a bit of time on this week that is not urgent, but important?

- What would it take to find the time to put towards one of those items?

Reframe moment!

You're not lazy; you've been aiming for a perfect that doesn't exist.

You're not lazy; you've been asking too much of yourself.

You're not lazy; you haven't had a chance to focus on your biggest priorities.

You're not lazy; it's time to outsource.

You're not lazy; it's time for more boundaries.

Reflection opportunity

How is your perfect different than other people's?

Is how you define perfect actually what *you* think is perfect or what you believe other people think would be perfect?

Believing in yourself is the magic solution

When I believe something is possible, the chances of it happening are about 1000 times higher than if I just hope it might happen for me.

Through my years of coaching (and coming on 50 years of living), I've noticed a consistent pattern regarding who easily achieves success.

People who believe in themselves and exude confidence find more success.

The more you believe something to be true, the more you speak about it confidently, the more likely you are to "go for it" and notice when opportunities appear.

Instead of confidence, we often fall into the trap of believing that we lack experience, fame, education, charisma, etc. Most often, that's simply not true. We aren't putting up our hands for things because we haven't believed in ourselves enough yet. We say we're lazy, but we're actually scared.

So let's talk about how to start believing more.

Manifesting through confidence

Full disclosure: when it comes to how much I believe in things I haven't seen proven by science I fall somewhere in the middle (this comes partially from having two parents with PhDs in science and engineering, I think!). I often try to insert a measure of logic into my magic.

When I hear people talking about manifesting, it tends to be either "it's the all-magical solution to *everything*" or "it is impossible." I believe the idea that saying you want a thing is all it takes to get that thing sets us up to feel bad. We may feel we didn't "do manifesting right" if it doesn't work out. Instead, I like to come at it from a middle ground. Let's be optimistic and intentional about the possibility that exists in the world so we can always take advantage of what is in front of us.

Regardless of what you might believe to be true when it comes to manifesting, here is something I've seen over and over again.

When you spend time thinking about

what you want and put words to it, you allow yourself to see it when it shows up.

The more you believe you will be able to do a thing or that a thing will happen, the more likely it is to happen.

There *is* likely some magic/energy/manifesting to this. But a huge part of it is just that you're willing to see it when it shows up.

It's incredible how much is constantly happening all around us that we aren't noticing. Our brains are powerful instruments that do a lot of work to filter out what we do and don't need without us ever being consciously aware of it. One of the most common examples of how this works is if you're thinking about buying a new kind of car, you suddenly notice them everywhere when you didn't before. It wasn't that they weren't there—you just didn't have a reason to notice them.

This is true with so many things, including opportunities. When you can give voice or words to the things you want to have to show up in the world, you're more likely to notice when they do. When you believe that you deserve those things you'll go for them with the confidence needed to succeed.

If you believe you deserve a promotion—truly believe it—your manager is more likely to believe you're ready than if you're nervous and unsure of whether or not you deserve it.

If you tell a potential client about a product or service and you think it's too expensive, that is very likely to come through in your voice, and they may also think it's too expensive. I've struggled more in selling something that costs $500 when I wasn't sure it was worth $500 than I have to sell something I confidently felt had great value and cost $10,000.

Sounds great Lara, but where shall I get this magical confidence and belief in myself of which you speak?

This is where it can be beneficial to spend some time practicing what it *feels* like to be confident. Spend some time journaling and ask yourself what it would feel like if you had ALL THE CONFIDENCE when it comes to that next thing you'd like to do. What would you say, how would you feel, what would your voice sound like?

Practice because the more you embody that feeling, the more comfortable you'll get and the more you'll start believing yourself.

Confidence *can* come from intentional creation, and it can make a huge difference in how we to reach our goals.

Challenge:

Pick someone in your life who believes in you. Now pretend you are them (even if it feels uncomfortable) and write 1-2 paragraphs about how good you are at something. It could be work, parenting, gardening, video games, anything.

If you're struggling with this exercise, go and ask someone who believes in you to write a paragraph or two about what you're great at. Actually—go do both!

Believing it will all work out in the end

My first job out of college was as the special events coordinator for a touristy part of my city. I hadn't yet fully discovered that "attention to detail" is not one of my skill sets, yet it was a *very* important requirement for someone with this job.

The position required me to take on many projects all at once, all of which required managing many small details. I was very bad at it. And I don't like being bad at things.

The incredible stress I felt while I had this job led me to have physical manifestations of the stress. Leading up to almost every single event I would get so tense that I couldn't turn my head to the left (which is especially tricky when setting up all the logistics for a massive neighbourhood event!)

I was miserable. My boss wasn't happy. It sucked.

Every day included small (or major!) mishaps —like forgetting the coffee urn for a coffee event, or dropping an envelope with $500 cash in the snow at night, or making mistakes with any of the one million small steps needed to coordinate the communications, people, and set-up of many events and activities to support local business owners!

I was always exhausted and knew I no longer wanted to work there. I spent hours daydreaming about quitting but could never find the capacity to do anything about it.

So I decided to quit. Even though I had rent to pay and no savings. Even though I didn't have enough money to cover more than a month of living expenses or any real idea how I would find more income. I knew that if I waited to have the energy to find a new job before quitting, I was more likely to have a nervous breakdown than actually to find a new job.

Everyone around me thought what I was doing was too risky and, honestly, stupid. But I felt confident that everything would be fine. I had NO question that it was the right next step for me.

Almost immediately, I got a couple of small contracts (my first toe-dipping into being a business owner). I got back in touch with the temping agencies I had worked for all through university and made a bit of money doing secretarial work. Then the person who had been my manager when I did my public relations internship found out that I had left my job and invited me to come and work for her.

In under the amount of time I had had savings for (which really was short), I secured a new full-time income that was a much better fit for me. I know there was some luck and a whole bunch of privilege involved here (and knew if needed there were people who could bail me out), but my belief that there would be a positive outcome allowed me to see what was possible.

The job I was given was as a secretary, and if I had decided the only thing that would be a good fit for me was in my field, I might have turned it down. Instead, I saw that a foot in as admin in a communications department was enough of a good step. And it did turn into the kind of job I wanted in under six months. Being open to what was possible was vital.

If I had waited to find another job before leaving my other job I probably would have been waiting for what looked like an ideal situation. Instead, my belief that things would work out landed me an opportunity that turned out to be ideal, even though on paper it didn't look it. I was ready for it and believed it would happen.

What you
BELIEVE IS POSSIBLE
helps make things possible.

Confidently advocating for yourself

In 2019 I got sick. Three times I got so sick that I ended up in the ER in more pain than I'd ever experienced (and I've had three babies).

Disclaimer: I'm about to talk UTERUSES! And that's another rule I'd like to challenge: the one that tells us we only talk about periods in hushed tones!

It turned out that I had severe and deep stage 4 endometriosis. Essentially endometriosis had destroyed my entire reproductive system and eaten up my appendix while it was at it. Starting one particular day in May 2019, I was in constant pain regardless of how many painkillers I took.

I was met with bad information (if I hadn't done my research and then had the confidence to stand up to doctors, I would have had very much the wrong treatment and would probably still be in pain), lack of knowledge (the number of doctors I met who told me they didn't know much about a disease that impacts at LEAST ten percent of women with uteruses is unconscionable), and I was told that it would take years to get the treatment I needed and there was no other option than for me to be patient and wait.

That's not what happened. I decided that that could not be my truth, and every cell in my body believed it.

I repeatedly asked doctors in the ER and my family doctor to advocate for me to get in to see the specialist I wanted to see over and over again. Eventually, one called to make a case for me to see him and got me in.

When the specialist gave me openings to plead my case further, no matter how small the opening was, I took it. I called the nurse and asked questions. I booked follow-up appointments and when the specialist said, "Why are you back here already?" instead of feeling guilty for wasting his time, I explained "I am in so much pain that I am exceeding your recommendations for a daily maximum dose. You told me to come back if that was the case, so here I am!" I didn't take less medication and deal. I didn't take more medication and keep quiet. I actively and confidently advocated for myself.

Despite being told it was impossible, I managed to get the best doctor in the city, have my first appointment moved up from six months to two months, and have my surgery date moved up from one year to two months.

My doctor told me that confidently using my voice was needed. He said he wished more women complained about endometriosis to the government the way men do about kidney stones. **Because confidently advocating for yourself makes a difference**.

I did have **VERY** advanced disease; the first thing my doctor said after surgery was, "If you were wondering if it was as bad as you thought in there—it was." (I *was* wondering. There's always that part of you that worries, right?)

I was lucky enough to have a family doctor willing to go to bat for me (to avoid me getting addicted to opioids.) The system is overburdened. Without some confidence advocating for yourself, you will have a million people step into the VIP line ahead of you as you wait.

And this holds true without having a terrible disease. I recently called to find out where I was on a waiting list for a small procedure and was booked in on the spot. I asked if I had missed a call, and she told me I hadn't. They were working their way through the list, but if people called in to check, it was nice and convenient for them to book those people in then. Politely waiting your turn instead of politely and confidently asking for updates and an opportunity to reach your goal can mean the difference between reaching it and not.

The same is true throughout your life—work, friends, health, etc. Politely advocating for yourself instead of patiently waiting is the middle ground between passive and pushy. Most of you reading this, like me, are probably people who have spent much of their life believing you should never be pushy. But a bit pushy to get your best outcome is A-okay!

When you believe that what you are asking for is reasonable and fair, it makes it easier to ask for, and people believe you when you explain things to them.

Reframe moment!

You're not lazy, you're scared.

You're not lazy, you're not sure what to do next.

You're not lazy, you've been conditioned to step back.

You're not lazy, you're waiting to feel more confident

Reflection opportunity

What do you wish you believed?

What would you do if you had more confidence?

The best way is your way

There is never only one way to do a thing.

Having three kids so close in age, including a set of twins, is an interesting way to see how much nature vs nurture is at play in life.

I always imagined parenting would get easier with more experience; I would know what to do as I gained confidence by referencing back to situations that would come up over and over again for each kid.

But here's what happened—I discovered each kid needed a different parenting experience. Because they were different, my husband and I needed to parent differently for each of them.

Despite them all growing up in almost identical circumstances with the same values and witnessing the same things (and how we modelled behaviour), all three of them not only have exceptionally different personalities but have different ways of feeling, processing, thinking, and very different motivations and priorities.

We have one social butterfly, one anxious caterpillar, and one independent cool cat.

We have some that are good at talking about their feelings and some that aren't. We have some that are great at self-entertaining and some that aren't. Some are more like me, so they trigger me, and we butt heads, and some do the same to my spouse. The one thing they all consistently did was rarely sleep as babies. #bigsigh.

Within our tiny ecosystem, we got three completely different results. Imagine what that means for all human beings. Our priorities, desires, motivations, strengths, and learning styles differ significantly from person to person. Yet we're all sent down the same life path, regardless of all those differences.

> Some people need hard deadlines to feel motivated; some people are crushed with anxiety by them.

> Some people need to read things; some people need to hear things.

> Some people thrive with rigid routines, and some feel claustrophobic with them.

> Some people like all the instructions before starting something, and others like to learn as they go.

> Some people love public speaking, and others love helping others get on stage.

We're taught that success looks a certain way.

What works for
OTHER PEOPLE
may not work for
YOU.

We're told that who we are as individuals doesn't impact that.

This is why so many people constantly feel bad about themselves and discouraged about how they're doing—they don't see themselves in the norms they're told they should meet, so they either have to change or give up.

Confidences get smashed. Dreams get crushed. And nobody tells us it's normal not to feel like that one perfect picture of success doesn't fit. That most people need to analyze and customize how things work for them to feel good. We all need to intentionally choose what success means and looks like for us.

So I'll tell you:

If what you're doing now isn't working, know there is almost certainly a different way to proceed other than "just do it!" When I hear "I'm just going to do it" from a client, it's a red flag for me. I know that they're almost always forcing something that isn't working and that it's time to find an alternative.

Reimagine, reframe, and reprioritize. When you figure out the right way for yourself as an individual, so much more is possible!

And if you need help with how to do that, know that you can find someone to support you the way YOU need to be supported, even if it's different from how your colleague, employee, bff, or sibling needs support.

And, if parenting is way more complicated than you ever thought—know that I get it! My kids push me daily to re-examine how I think things should be and ask myself what the best way for all of us is to move forward.

Memory styles

Do you prefer to read a paper book, an e-book or listen to an audiobook? You may even like to read the Coles Notes (or the audio-equivalent, Blinkist) because you like your information in short bursts, not in long form.

How we receive and process information differs, and that's okay.

I receive information better when I listen to it while also doing another low-thought task (like driving, doing dishes, taking notes or doodling, etc.)

Other people struggle to receive information auditorily, and it works much better for them to have visuals to help anchor the information in their brains.

And yet another group of people do best when they learn by doing.

Those three-hour lectures with only one break I had in university with a professor *talking at* 500 students weren't the most effective way to learn for most people—shocking right?

Virtual learning has been something that some students have taken to like it's the best thing that ever existed, and others struggle more than ever before. And the thing is, nobody is right or wrong—there are so many ways that people can learn, and most of the time learning styles aren't factored into the teaching process.

So first, if you find yourself struggling, you need to acknowledge that there are differences in learning, and it's not just about "getting your act together." Then you get to start figuring out the best ways for you to learn.

Let's talk about some of the ways you might be doing things more differently than you even realize.

There are a million ways to do something

One day on Facebook, someone posted a simple math problem and asked people how they solved it. It asked, "What happens in your brain when you solve this?"

The problem was 27 + 48 (stop here solve in your head before continuing).

I loved this question and the answers so much that I shared the problem on my Facebook profile. The 100+ comments told me other people find this as fascinating as I do.

The way I answered this question was:

48 + 7 = 55 + 20 = 75

Other answers included :

2 + 4 = 6(0), then 7 + 8 = 15, then 60 + 15

68 + 2 + 5

20 + 40 is 60, then add 7 + 8

7 + 8 is 15, add it to 20+40

25 + 50

27 + 50 and then subtract 2

27 plus 48

30 + 50 - 5

And "the answer just popped into my head!"

Every one of those answers is correct, but the way the answer was processed happened in many different ways. Were some ways faster? Maybe. But in all cases, how their brain processed the information was legitimate and worked.

Sometimes we get stuck thinking there is a "right way to do a thing." What if that wasn't true?

Instead of thinking, "I was supposed to do it the way I was taught in class," what if we all embraced that maybe we have a different way? A way that we like better or can remember. And whether or not it was the *correct* way to get to the right answer doesn't matter.

Let's keep going with math examples (a subject I did not excel in at school). One day when my kid was in fourth grade, they came home with a math problem my husband was trying to help with. Throughout my relationship with my husband, he's regularly been amused by how I tackle a math or numbers problem differently than he does. He tells people that I do math in a backwards twisty way. When he was trying to help our kid with this homework, the only way he could think to solve the problem was with algebra. He realized that couldn't be what they were expecting for fourth grade, so he called on me to do "my" kind of math.

I could figure out the answer in a few seconds because I've always done math in my head by taking apart numbers and then putting them back together (which is what new math is all about, and I think it's excellent, no matter how odd it is compared to what we were learning in school in the last century!). That was the simple way to look at this particular problem, and my way of looking at it was perfect.

Algebra and calculus are great and important tools, but you don't always need to use the big guns. Getting too stuck on "how math works" can sometimes be limiting. How I thought about numbers and math was far more helpful than my husband's understanding of it in that moment.

This same thing holds for many things in life. Take the path that feels good for you to figure things out. Don't judge yourself for not doing it the "right" way or for not remembering how it's "supposed" to be done. We spend so much time worrying about the parts we got wrong that we don't celebrate what we got right and how we're doing.

I want you to celebrate what's working.

I want you to see how your way of thinking could be different, but that doesn't mean there's anything wrong with it.

What the hobbits taught me about my brain

In university, I took a Children's Literature class. We read all kinds of classics like *Charlotte's Web*, *Gulliver's Travels* and, most importantly for telling this story, *The Hobbit*.

If you've read Tolkien's writing, it is descriptive in the extreme and revered by many for exactly that reason. Here is a little bit of the first chapter of *The Hobbit*:

> *In a hole in the ground there lived a hobbit. Not a nasty, dirty, wet hole, filled with the ends of worms and an oozy smell, nor yet a dry, bare, sandy hole with nothing in it to sit down on or to eat: it was a hobbithole, and that means comfort.*
>
> *It had a perfectly round door like a porthole, painted green, with a shiny yellow brass knob in the exact middle. The door opened on to a tubeshaped hall like a tunnel: a very comfortable tunnel without smoke, with panelled walls, and floors tiled and carpeted,*

provided with polished chairs, and lots and lots of pegs for hats and coats the Hobbit was fond of visitors. The tunnel wound on and on, going fairly but not quite straight into the side of the hill - The Hill, as all the people for many miles round called it and many little round doors opened out of it, first on one side and then on another. No going upstairs for the Hobbit: bedrooms, bathrooms, cellars, pantries (lots of these), wardrobes (he had whole rooms devoted to clothes), kitchens, dining rooms, all were on the same floor, and indeed on the same passage.

When I read this book, I complained endlessly to anyone who would listen about how descriptive it was, how much of a waste of time it felt like, and how *boring* it was.

During these conversations, I would hear how much other people appreciated just how skilled Tolkien was at painting a picture with words. The level of details he included in his books brings alive the scenes he creates in people's brains.

What was my problem, then? Why was I skipping over more than half the paragraphs and wishing Tolkien could just GET TO THE POINT!? I couldn't understand why he felt the need to tell me about every aspect of the road and the trees and the smells in the forest when he could say "big forest, rocky path" and be done with it.

It was during that class that I realized I could *not* bring the images he created into my brain the way other people could. I couldn't visualize his story, but other people could. I was disappointed, but didn't spend much time thinking about this difference.

It wasn't until decades later that I truly understood how differently I was processing information when I heard about something called "aphantasia."

Aphantasia is the inability to bring up images in your brain. For some, it is also the inability to bring up smells and sounds in their minds. While there is some talk of this phenomenon dating back to the 1800s, it wasn't until 2015 that Dr Adam Zeman gave it the name aphantasia. Until then, many people thought it was really rare and unusual. It turns out it's far more common than people thought and that without a conversation that allowed people to truly describe their experiences, most people didn't know they were processing information differently.

Without conversation, we assume we're all thinking the same way. It turns out that's not true. Once people started talking about it, both sides were shocked that the other was experiencing something completely different.

Those who *could* visualize would ask a million questions including, "How do you even remember things?!" and those who couldn't visualize wondered, "Is it like you're on some kind of acid trip 24/7 with images flying around distracting you? That sounds very overwhelming!"

Understanding that people think and process

differently is hugely important because it can change their experience entirely.

Every time I'm at an event or participating in an activity that starts with, "close your eyes and picture in your mind… a beach, your best life, how it would look, feel, smell, sound…" the room can probably hear my eyes roll back into my head.

Why? Because I am thinking, "Great… another activity I can't do." It makes me sad, like I'm missing out on something or wasting my time.

But here's the thing—I'm super creative. I have a great memory. I also have a great imagination (it just isn't visual!) Not being able to hear, see and smell things in my mind doesn't hamper my ability to do most things in life (other than being able to pull things up in my mind, which sounds kind of amazing and I won't deny being a bit sad I can't do it).

What it highlights to me is how differently the brain works for different people. We all have different brains. We have different ways of learning, processing, and creating. That means there can't ever be one way to teach people, ask them to do tasks, or to motivate them.

I often tell people about aphantasia, partially because everyone thinks it's so interesting, but even more importantly because it lets them know there are opportunities to adapt their language to be more inclusive to those who don't process information the way they do. Understanding that we aren't all thinking and processing information the same way helps us both be more compassionate of ourselves and more supportive of others.

I also talk about it because so many people finally realize why they are so frustrated when people ask them to visualize. They have aphantasia too and didn't know! Normalizing how different we all are can be one of the greatest gifts you can give people.

By recognizing that most of us think and operate differently, we can stop being so hard on ourselves when things don't work. We can also be more understanding of others. By trying to have options for the different ways people think, you are also opening up a world of opportunities simply by being inclusive.

Try not to get discouraged when something isn't working for you. Instead ask yourself, what *does* work for you?

The brain is fascinating. We need to recognize how it works for all of us differently, and that that's not a bad thing.

Are you starting from the same starting line?

For all that we give ourselves a hard time about how we don't measure up to anyone else, one of the things we rarely acknowledge is whether we're starting from the same place as everyone else.

As someone who has struggled with chronic pain and fatigue for decades, I hear the constant messages from society that the key to success is to "just do it" and that "it isn't that hard." They just made me feel tired, sick, and bad about myself.

Whether we're talking physically or mentally, there are many ways that we aren't starting from the same place as everyone else, and we need to acknowledge that.

I took an assessment for sensory sensitivity, where you would answer with a range from "all the time" to "none of the time." One of the questions asked was how often I like to move my body, and I immediately thought, "none of the time!"

Moving my body takes a lot of work. I don't trust it to do the things I know I will want to do. I walk into doorways, get tired on walks, and exercise never feels good (no matter how often I've been told the endorphins and joy will come—not for me!)

What it takes for me to get up and do the physical activity is not the same as what it takes for someone who gets a lot of good feelings from moving their body. I'm not saying I won't do it anyways, but I can't measure my effort fairly against someone who loves to work out.

When you wonder why someone wouldn't just do the thing you find easy or fun, ask yourself if maybe it isn't easy or fun for that person. Imagine how you feel when your body is weak after a bad cold and how you would feel if that was your baseline. Would that change how you view the effort someone else is putting in?

Let me share another physical example. After I had COVID-19 my snoring got so bad that I started using a CPAP machine to help me breathe at night. I have been chronically tired since I was a teenager. It has *never* been easy for me to wake up. If I woke up feeling rested a handful of times over a year, I was doing quite well.

For me, waking up has felt like travelling through molasses to get to the real world. Once awake, my brain and body still needed lots of time to start moving and operating properly.

After a couple of weeks of using the CPAP machine, I started to wake up and think, "Okay. I'm awake". That's it. It isn't painful. It doesn't require Herculean effort, I'm just awake (though I am still sleepy/groggy.)

That means that for all those years where I couldn't wake up without it being painful, I was starting from a different place than people who could wake up quickly. I didn't realize what it felt like to wake without effort (it's nice, by the way!).

It's easy to think people are lazy when they aren't doing things you think are simple. When we acknowledge that we all have different experiences we can be kinder to ourselves and to others.

I'm not done going on about this yet; let's talk about how it impacts us in even more ways.

The same holds true for bravery

Over the years, I've shared many stories of my life (of my ADHD diagnosis, endometriosis and many others) with people, and often I get told I'm very brave for sharing those stories.

Here's the secret about me sharing all those things. It required no bravery from me. It wasn't scary. The stories came out easily and without fear. What it would take for you to share the same level of your life might be entirely different from what it took me.

The level of bravery it takes to tell many of my stories is... none. For whatever reason, probably a combination of a tendency to overshare and the belief that sharing is helping people, and the fact that I've done so much work on releasing shame from my life, it isn't hard to share this stuff.

Being brave is being able to do something that takes courage. Courage is doing something that scares you.

It was brave for me to get up on stage and do

stand-up comedy back in 2019. It wasn't nearly as brave for me to tell people all about my ADHD and endometriosis because it felt like information everyone would (or in my opinion "should") be happy to receive. It didn't feel like something shameful or scary to me.

What requires courage and bravery for each of us is different. I think calling and ordering food directly from the restaurant when I'm tired and emotional takes more bravery than telling everyone about my uterus, but that may not be the same for you.

Honour the fact that what takes courage and bravery for each of us is different. Please don't measure yourself by others when you don't know where they're starting from.

The same holds for privilege

I want to make sure I acknowledge that what is easy for me often comes from my privilege—and I have a lot of it. I grew up with supportive parents who made a good salary and got me a lot of backing when needed. I have a very supportive spouse who earns an income which means I have more safety in some of the decisions I make in my business than others would. Where I'm starting from isn't the same as it is for everyone else, so don't measure yourself up to me or anyone else.

It's easy to think you must be lazy if everyone keeps telling you your behaviour is lazy. We internalize what society thinks, and now we not only feel bad we didn't do <insert thing>, we feel bad about ourselves.

Reframe moment!

You're not lazy, you're starting from a different baseline.

You're not lazy, you're trying to do something really scary.

You're not lazy, you're comparing yourself to someone in totally different circumstances.

You're not lazy, your brain works differently.

You're not lazy, society is setting you up to feel badly about yourself.

Reflection opportunity

How do you do things differently than others?

Are there things that people seem to understand
that has always seemed harder for you?

What can you give yourself a little more compassion for?

The resistance is real

I know that some of you reading this book are going to have internalized the feeling of being less-than more than others. If you're feeling like a bit of a hot mess who can't possibly be who this book was meant for, this part is for you.

You may feel like a mess—I know that I regularly do.

But life is messy. I'm okay with that and you can be too. I can be messy, emotional, and unorganized, which doesn't mean I'm not still great at things. I'm great at being a mom, wife, and friend. I feel successful in what I do and I'm financially stable.

Messy isn't necessarily bad—it can be the beautiful chaos from which creativity, art, and magic are born.

Being messy some of the time doesn't mean that you're messy all of the time. Being messy can mean that you're feeling your feelings and not spending your life pretending to be strong when you aren't (and none of us are meant to be strong all of the time). You're being authentic and not trying to hide. That's not a bad thing.

Being late, indecisive or wearing clothing that seems to clash doesn't mean that you have any less value or ability than anybody else.

I used to spend my life feeling like the kind of hot mess I didn't want anyone to *know* about. All my feelings felt like dirty little secret that I would forget to complete tasks, that I wasn't making as much money as people thought, and that I wasn't always loving my work. The shame I was carrying around was at the root of my frequent decision paralysis, my tendency to make lists that I would never complete, and my inability to meet most of the goals I set for myself.

Once I started to let people in—to let them know when I make mistakes (without all the angst), and to let them in when I felt vulnerable, I stopped feeling like such a mess. So many people appreciated and thanked me for being real and thanked me for modelling being authentic that I started to believe in myself.

All the things that I worried made me a mess didn't go away; I just stopped believing they made me "less than".

I hope that as you read this book, you saw all the ways that owning the ups and downs that come with being you doesn't mean that you aren't able to be successful. I hope you can see how letting go of a lot of the shame that comes with feeling like a hot mess all the time could be life-changing. If it feels like this might be true for other people but not for you, know that you deserve this grace too. Also, know that it can take time to learn to be self-accepting. Noticing the resistance you have in changing how you think about things is precisely that, resistance.

Together we can normalize being real people with real feelings and real lives to juggle. Sometimes it's just too much to do all the things—and that's not a failure. Sometimes we aren't going to love something we loved the day before—that's part of life and being a human. It doesn't mean we made a mistake.

Whether you feel like a disaster or not actually doesn't impact your success.

I believe in you. My biggest hope for you from reading this book is that you believe in yourself more than you did when you began. Life isn't about suddenly feeling like a grown-up who has everything together; it's about knowing how to keep moving through the moments when you don't.

You're not lazy; you're amazing just the way you are. You can do incredible things.

Now what?

Thank you for taking this journey with me. The messages I've included in this book are ones that over the years, people have kept telling me revolutionize how they think about work and rest.

If these messages resonated with you and you're ready to start reframing how you feel about who you are, how you get things done and what can come next, keep journeying with me. You can find resources, videos, and stories on the You're Not Lazy web page. Come and hang out with me so we can keep unpacking all of this stuff together. You can find all the ways to do that at www.yourenotlazy.ca

Take your time going through the many journaling prompts in the book (if you're like me, you didn't do them as you went and have forgotten that you meant to go back to them).

Give yourself some grace and compassion, and keep remembering we've been taught to see ourselves as all kinds of broken and not good enough. I hope to be the voice in your head reminding you that it's okay not to be the way you thought everyone wanted you to be.

I'm sending you so much love and compassion, and above all remember, you're not lazy!

Acknowledgements

For a book about letting things be easy and not making them harder than they have to be, I did not find writing it easy. It took me four years from start to finish, and it changed topics and audiences and key messages many times. I had to remind myself often to let it be easier, and that the challenge would be worth it when I got to the end. Having finally arrived at this place where I am done, I can truly say that I learned so much going through this, and I am glad I pushed through the discomfort. I am also glad beyond measure to have had so many people helping me along the way!

Darlene Turriff and Nicole Washburn – thank you for holding my hand while I got this book out of "one day" and into now. I wouldn't have gotten it done if it weren't for our weekly calls.

Marie, Julie, Robin, and Marsha – thank you for letting me share your stories in this book. And thank you for being early readers and confirming this book is something the world needs (something I really needed to hear when I was struggling with the book!)

Amanda Spencer – thank you for this book cover. I knew you would get inside my brain and figure out the perfect cover almost by magic, and that's exactly what you did.

To my amazing clients who trust me with so much of what is happening in their work and personal lives, thank you! I guide you, but I also learn from you, and you are the reason I know so much of what I have experienced and learned is helpful to many others. Thousands of hours of coaching reinforced in me the need for this book out in the world.

I have such amazing friends – Erin, Vicky, Alison, Karen, and Misty; thank you for listening when I wanted to philosophize or had book things on the brain.

To my parents – thank you for being so supportive of me my whole life and trusting me to find my path even when it seemed pretty risky or out in left field.

Kiernan, Quinn, and Juliette – you inspire and teach me how to be more myself every day. Keep being yourselves - you're amazing. I love you, my kiddos.

The biggest thank you goes to my husband, Eric, who had to live with me as I rode the rollercoaster of emotions I had about this book. He sat with me to make edits when I was feeling particularly frustrated or overwhelmed, stopped me from deleting entire chapters out of frustration, and took on the job of laying out the book so I could release the stress of being done before starting to see the book in book format. Thank you for always believing I can do the random things I decide I want to do and lending me some of that belief when I start to doubt myself.

Glossary

Definitions (according to me and how I use them) of words/terms found in this book

ADHD

Attention Deficit Hyperactivity Disorder. This is the blanket term used for what most think of both ADHD and ADD. It can present in many different ways. I received my diagnosis at 40.

Aphantasia

An inability to create mental images, sounds or smells. Until quite recently, most of us with aphantasia mostly thought you weren't being literal when you said, "picture this."

Emotional regulation

Being able to respond to things in a "typical" and socially acceptable way. When we are tired, stressed, or just out of sorts we struggle with emotional regulation.

Endometriosis

A disease that at least one in ten people with uteruses have that can cause infertility and incredible pain. It is not well understood and there is not enough research done on the topic or doctors who specialize in treating it.

Hot mess

A particularly disorganized person who seems to barely be holding it together.

Lazy

Not a thing. Let's stop using it.

Mindset

How you think about things. A lot of what we cover in this book is going to be about the things you think, and how you might want to start re-programming those thoughts to new ones that are kinder and gentler.

Neurodivergent

Those who are not seen as typical when it comes to mental and neurological function. Often used for those with ADHD, Autism, Dyslexia, Dyspraxia, and other cognitive variations.

Toxic positivity

Pushing positivity so hard you don't acknowledge things that aren't positive. Life isn't always positive and that's okay.

Triggered

Having an emotional reaction in response to something someone has done or said or that has happened.

People mentioned in this book

Brené Brown – brenebrown.com

Glennon Doyle – momastery.com

Jonathan Fields – jonathanfields.com

Marie Forleo – marieforleo.com

Gay Hendricks – hendricks.com

Terry Matlen – addconsults.com

Jessica McCabe – howtoadhd.com

Marsha Shandur – yesyesmarsha.com

Marie Shinmoto – mapphysiotherapy.ca

Robin Whitford – hookingoutsidethelines.com

Laura Wright – laurawrightofficial.com